THE COMPLETE BOOK OF
COMBAT
HANDGUNNING

BY
CHUCK
TAYLOR

The Complete Book of Combat Handgunning
by Chuck Taylor

Copyright © 1982 by Chuck Taylor

ISBN 13: 978- 0-87364-327-6
Printed in the United States of America

Published by Paladin Press, a division of
Paladin Enterprises, Inc.
Gunbarrel Tech Center
7077 Winchester Circle
Boulder, Colorado 80301 USA
+1.303.443.7250

Direct inquiries and/or orders to the above address.

PALADIN, PALADIN PRESS, and the
are trademarks belonging to Paladin Enterprises and
registered in United States Patent and Trademark Office.

Visit our Web site at www.paladin-press.com

Table Of Contents

AUTHOR'S NOTE V

FOREWORD By Chris McLoughlin VII

CHAPTER 1:   HISTORIC PERSPECTIVE 1
                    Cause And Effect

CHAPTER 2:   THE PURPOSE OF THE HANDGUN 7
                    Much Abused And Misunderstood

CHAPTER 3:   CARE AND CLEANING 13
                    A Critical Influence Upon Reliability

CHAPTER 4:   PREPARING THE HANDGUN FOR COMBAT 21
                    Modifications That Bring Out Its Full Potential

CHAPTER 5:   HOLSTERS & SPARE AMMUNITION CARRIERS . . 41
                    Important Accessories

CHAPTER 6:   HANDGUN STOPPING POWER 57
                    The Name Of The Game

CHAPTER 7:   TECHNIQUE 79
                    How To Best Utilize The Defensive Handgun

CHAPTER 8:   COMBAT HANDGUNNING TACTICS 111
                    The Basics Of Survival

CHAPTER 9:   MENTAL CONDITIONING 125
                    Alertness Minimizes Danger

CHAPTER 10: TRAINING & COMPETITION 129

REFERENCE SECTION 141
                  GLOSSARY: Terminologies & Definitions 143
                  Handgun Nomenclature 155
                  Arms Importers & Manufacturers 156
                  Accessories — Where To Find Them 158
                  Handgun Related Materials (Publications) 163
                  Principal Military Handguns Of The World 165
                  Custom Gunsmith Directory 167
                  Ammo Data: .45 ACP & 9mm Parabellum 169
                  Pro-Gun Editorial 171

Author's Note

The subject matter covered herein is both abstract and diverse. It is the subject of intense controversy and contradiction, as well as heated debate.

In what follows, I hope to place in proper perspective for the reader the basic fundamentals, as well as the philosophies behind them, of the grim but necessary business of defending with a handgun one's self against unexpected attack from without. The facts stated and opinions rendered are derived from a lifetime of combat experience as well as an intense effort into research, interview, and experimentation and are set forth on this basis.

It is hoped that the reader will understand that those opinions are intended in the spirit of saving lives. I have no "axe to grind" with anyone, but feel strongly that any fallacies that exist within the field must be defined, along with an explanation of why they are dangerous. Were I not to pursue this conviction I would be guilty of both hypocrisy and unprofessionalism, neither of which are acceptable conditions to me.

Special thanks goes to Chris McLoughlin, who, in addition to much else, honored me by writing the foreword contained on page VII, and to his beautiful wife Connie. Without their active encouragement and assistance this book never would have seen fruition.

Last, I dedicate the book to "M" and "T" . . . whose presence in my life illustrated to me that there are indeed some things that are worth fighting, and, if necessary, even dying for.

Chuck Taylor
Atlanta, Georgia
December 1981

Foreword

Chuck Taylor surprised me more than just a little when he asked that I write the foreword to this, his first book. In Taylor's world, his peers are so much more eminently qualified than I on the subject of firearms, that I am honored to have been selected as herald for these legions.

To begin with, you must realize that this book is unashamedly honest, and it must be in order to make clear the points that may save your life in a gunfight. Taylor is an articulate man with a wry sense of humor that is interspersed throughout this work. He is cynical, but not offensive while calling a spade a spade. The knowledge and experience that has given him the right to do so has been earned and his credentials are impeccable.

In 1965 Taylor joined the Army and in that year he finished Advanced Infantry Training. By 1967 he completed Infantry Officer Training School and Ranger training. He holds Military Expert Ratings with the .45 ACP M1911 pistol, 5.56mm M-16 rifle, 7.62mm M-14 rifle, .30 M-1 Carbine, 7.62 M-60 machine gun and 40mm M-79 grenade launcher. During 18 months' service in Vietnam, Taylor earned these decorations: Vietnam Service, Vietnam Campaign with five stars, the Bronze Star with "V" device, Vietnamese Cross of Gallantry with Palm, Combat Infantryman's Badge and the Purple Heart. He retired from the service with the rank of Captain, O-3, and that commission is still held. With these military qualifications as a basis, Taylor achieved civilian Expert ratings in NRA Light Rifle, High Power Carbine and High Power Rifle. He is an NRA Certified Rifle and Pistol Instructor, has held an IPSC Class A rating since 1976, and was a member of the 1978-1979 IPSC United States Team.

Taylor's work here deals with competition shooting in situations where life and survival are the only prizes. Olympian obstacle courses of fire and sideshow shooting are not within the scope of things treated here. He does not shoot dimes or aspirin tablets out of the air, nor does he split bullets on edged weapons and break balloons with the halves. Instead, the demonstrations of his skills are more mundane. Recently he displayed almost uncanny expertise in a Demi-*Presidente* (a 180° turn, draw, two shots on each of three silhouette targets 10 meters downrange, reload, and one shot on each of the heads of the targets) — a perfect score in 6.2 seconds! In that same demonstration he placed four consecutive center hits with a 12 gauge pump shotgun on four silhouette targets at 7 yards — in 1.5 seconds. With the submachine gun set in full auto mode, Taylor places single center hits on the heads of silhouette targets in 1.5 seconds. This is a remarkable testimonial to his trigger control amd overall weapon control. Even so, these accomplishments alone do not make him an expert, for they are merely manifestations of a highly honed skill. The fact that Taylor has survived not just one but numerous gun battles based almost solely on his individual ability is a far more significant factor.

Detached objectivity (it is said that a professional takes his work seriously, not himself) has played a key role in the development of Taylor's personal shooting skills and his ability to pass them along to others. These are the marks of the expert, the professional. Fundamental shooting skills, honed by hours of repetitious practice, have tested true for Taylor. Beyond that, theory has been put to task; shortcomings have been rejected and successes are advanced and elevated to applications which are now absolutes representing state-of-the-art development. Readers who are familiar with handgun technique will notice certain subtle refinements in techniques, and they may look askance before testing them out for themselves. Let me assure you that these changes are made for progress, not merely for the sake of change. Taylor is not subject to the feelings of insecurity that fosters the revamping of a system to carve an image for self-identification. Again I emphasize that these improvements are the result of strong basics and an open mindedness to the reality of modern day problems that require solutions, not just responses. These are improvements that have saved Taylor's life and the lives of his students.

Jeff Cooper declared Chuck Taylor a *Master Marksman* early in 1979 when he joined the staff at the American Pistol Institute as Operations Manager and Senior Instructor. That tenure of office was terminated in the latter part of 1980, and it was shortly after that time when Taylor founded the American Small Arms Academy. Now operating under that banner, Taylor has become one of the most sought-after shooting instructors in the world, not only by civilians from all walks of life, but from elite organizations throughout the Free World. Africa and Latin America have felt the impact of his work as a small arms consultant, and members of many SWAT and TRU teams, U.S. military (Special Forces/Ranger) units, the Rhodesian SAS, Israeli Army and German GSG-9 are alive today as a result of his tactical training with the combat handgun and special weapons. Taylor became the only known *Four Weapon Master* (rifle, shotgun, submachine gun and handgun) in 1981.

It is clear that Taylor has elevated handgunning to a new level: that of a discipline for self-defense and personal protection, as are other martial arts and sciences that are applicable to the control of our environments. His teachings inspire pride and confidence in one's self and one's accomplishments with the handgun. The weapon is taught with an eye to the dignity owed a tool, an object of pleasure and an instrument of life.

CHRIS McLOUGHLIN
Associate Editor
Combat Handguns Magazine

Responsibility is a unique concept. It can only reside and inhere in a single individual. You may share it with others, but your portion is not diminished. You may delegate it, but it is still with you. You may disclaim it, but you cannot divest yourself of it. Even if you do not recognize it or recognize its presence, you cannot escape it. If responsibility is rightfully yours, no evasion or ignorance, or passing the blame can shift the burden on someone else. Unless you can point your finger at the man who is responsible when something goes wrong, then you never had anyone really responsible.

Vice Admiral Hyman G. Rickover
15 June 1961

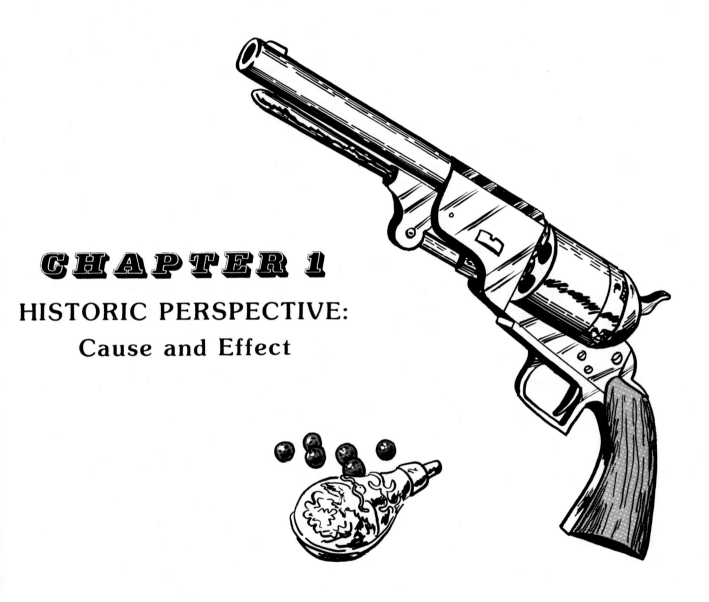

CHAPTER 1
HISTORIC PERSPECTIVE:
Cause and Effect

Although the handgun in a usable form had been in existence for at least several hundred years, it was not until about 1831 that it achieved the status of being a truly effective personal weapon. Up until this time, all handguns had been relegated to the mission of a tactical curiosity inasmuch as the lack of sustained fire, as well as an excess of accessory equipment to load and maintain the weapon being required, precluded them from reaching their full potential.

It is certainly true that, while certain examples of the *status quo* single shot handgun existed in potent calibers, the lack of repeat shot capability caused it to be discarded in favor of the time-proven saber or lance during cavalry operations. Moreover, the cumbersome size of the representative weapons of the day hardly constituted a portable, or convenient for that matter, package for daily carry and use.

The technology of firearms also had great negative influence on the situation because of metallurgy flaws and the difficulty of obtaining spare parts, etc. Indeed, a fellow finding himself alone on the Great Plains of the United States armed with a

Early use of the Colt revolver occurred during the Mexican Wars of the early Texas frontier when **hardy settlers and adventurers frequently clashed with Mexican troops.**

broken handgun found little solace in the fact that everyone else armed with a handgun had the same problem! Considering the fact that the handgun was almost never used except in a defensive role, a malfunction or broken gun usually meant death to the party to whom the weapon belonged. Thus, the reputation of the arm was less than sterling, to say the least! — And, the conventional military weapons, the sword and lance, continued to dominate the field of close-in action, while the musket and newer rifle remained in control of the more distant scenarios.

Samuel Colt emerged as the man who was destined to contribute one of the most significant improvements in the handgun's history and, at the same time because of his improvements, allow the great Western expansion of 1850-1880 to take place. Specifically, the problem with the handgun in single shot form was that it was only effective for a short period of time, upon which, when the single shot was expended, the firer was forced to unpack his accessory paraphernalia and attempt to render

the weapon reloaded and back into service. Unfortunately, those toward whom the firer's hostilities were directed normally chose this opportunity to attack with their own weapon(s). Thus, in order to retain anything approaching a modicum of tactical flexibility, the firer was forced to carry a quantity of handguns and/or abandon the weapon in favor of the saber, once the single shot was expended.

The Colt repeating handgun, pioneered in a usable form by the .31 caliber Paterson revolver, allowed a single man to become a serious problem inside 100 yards because now that single man had a sustained fire capability, as well as increased range potential. The old tactic of causing a victim to fire his pistol, then dashing in to chop him up with an edged weapon was suddenly and decisively rendered suicidal, as a great many Plains Indians quickly discovered! To compound his firepower, a man could even carry two revolvers, which effectively doubled his newly found field superiority. He could also increase his firepower by carrying spare, loaded cylinders for his revolver(s). Needless to say, the empty cylinder could be exchanged for a loaded one in a fraction of the time that it could be reloaded.

The Paterson was improved into a more robust and potent arm and Colt truly "arrived" when the prestigious Texas Rangers, then fighting Indians in Texas under the flamboyant Captain Jack Hayes, obtained a quantity of Colt's revolvers and began actually using them in both mounted and dismounted combat. Letters in Colt's files attested to the overwhelming acceptance and superiority of his six-guns:

"I have just received a pair of Colt's pistols which he sent to me as a present. There is not an officer who has seen them but speaks in the highest terms of them and all of the Cavalry officers are determined to get them if possible. Col. Harney says they are the best arm in the world. They are as effective as the common rifle at one hundred yards and superior to a musket even at two hundred yards.
S. H. Walker"

The radical change in combative philosophies was summed up nicely by the Rangers:

"Those prairie tribes ride with boldness and wonderful skill, and are, perhaps, unsurpassed, as irregular cavalry. They are so dexterous in the use of the bow, that a single Indian, at full speed, is capable of keeping an arrow constantly in the air, between himself and the enemy, therefore, to encounter such an expert antagonist, with any certainty of doing execution, requires an impetuous charge, skillful horsemanship, and a rapid discharge of shots, such as can only be delivered with Colt's six-shooters."

The Rangers' imposing S. H. Walker, being of a mechanical bent himself, even suggested improvements to increase the power, range, and reliability of Colt's revolvers, many of which were enthusiastically accepted by Colt and incorporated into subsequent models. The huge .44 "Walker Colt" became a decided success in the heats of many battles in many places, even far outside the confines of the Texas plains. Speaking of the Walker, Senator William Gwin of California opined:

"The Indians of the gorges of the Sierra Nevada are terrified into honest habits, by the miners in that region being armed with these pistols."

It wasn't long, even after repeated attempts to ignore Colt's revolvers, that the U.S. Army began to take notice. Captain S. G. French, Assistant Quartermaster of the Army and a veteran of both the Texas and Mexican campaigns, stated:

"Such confidence was reposed in those pistols that whenever I had occasion to send small parties in advance, or to employ express riders to carry the mails through Indian country, it was always made a condition, that they should be furnished with Colt's revolvers; otherwise they would not risk their lives in such service."

Eventually, the U.S. Army, in 1860 via a board of examining officers, paid the ultimate tribute to Colt's guns by reporting:

Captain S. H. Walker, frequent correspondent of Samuel Colt and the man who worked closely with Colt to develop the revolver into a heavy duty service handgun.

The handgun has always been a cherished trophy of the military battlefield, for not-always sentimental reasons! Here a U.S. Army bugler checks his M1873 Colt .45 SA revolver during the Moro campaigns of the late 1800's.

"The superiority of Colt's revolvers, as an arm for cavalry operations, which has been so well established, is now finally confirmed by the production of the new model with the 8 inch barrel. There are a few minor points requiring modification, to which the manufacturer's notice has been called, and to which he should be required to attend in all arms of the kind he may furnish for Government use . . . the Board are satisfied that the New Model Revolver with the 8 inch barrel will make the most superior cavalry arm we have ever had and they recommend the adoption of this New Model and its issue to all the mounted troops."

The chairman of the board was J. E. Johnston, who in only a few months would resign his com-

mission to join the Confederate Army and compile an outstanding record as the best defensive general in the entire Confederate Army.

As the Civil War drew to a conclusion, Westward migration recommenced and the Colt revolver again found itself in the midst of guerrilla warfare activities mounted against the whites by the Indians of the West. General Harney of the U.S. Army declared:

"I consider the arm perfect for the dragoon service, particularly when opposed to the Western Prairie Indians. It is the only weapon with which we can hope ever to subdue those wild and daring tribes . . ."

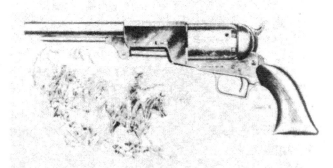

The massive .44 caliber Walker Colt revolver.

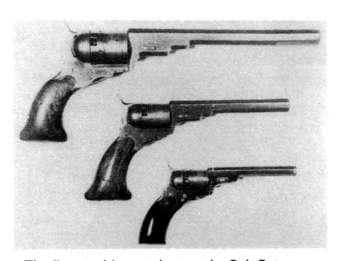

The first working revolvers — the Colt Patersons.

In 1873 another quantum leap was facilitated by Colt, who, in spite of the lifelong refusal of Sam Colt himself to accept the concept, produced the famous Single Action Army caliber .45 revolver, utilizing a metallic cartridge instead of retaining the percussion fired concept of its predecessors. Fortunately for Colt, Smith & Wesson had refrained

Late 1800's advertisement for metallic cartridge conversions of the Colt M1851 Navy and M1860 Army. Replicas of these guns, in percussion form, are popular with black powder shooters today.

from manufacturing their cartridge revolvers in large service calibers, thus the new Colt was a smashing success in the field and was quickly adopted by the military and civilian communities alike and remained in service until the 1890's.

Towards the end of the century, the advent of smokeless powder allowed the consummation of many self-operating designs that had been previously impractical because of black powder's fouling tendencies and names like Borchardt, Luger and Browning signalled the coming of the self-loading weapon. Beginning in 1896 with the "Broomhandle Mauser", the so-called "automatic pistol" began to lead the way in handgun development, while the still-popular revolver began to slip a bit.

Browning's great M1911 auto pistol is clearly the most significant milestone in combative handgun development of this century even though it occurred in 1911. Unsurpassed as a personal defense handgun, it has compiled the most phenomenal record of success in history and continues to ride the crest of its unparalleled popularity even after 70 years!

Efforts by Douglas Wesson and Elmer Keith pioneered the development of the so-called "magnum" handguns and cartridges which appeared, beginning with the .357 Magnum in 1935, the .44 Magnum in 1956 and the .41 Magnum, this time with the assistance of Bill Jordan, in 1964. While interesting technological achievements, the "magnum revolution" was mostly an excellent means of

The Browning designed, Colt manufactured M1911 .45 caliber self-loading pistol, the gun many feel to be the best fighting handgun ever built.

advertising for the firearms and ammunition manufacturers and actually had very little effect upon the development of defensive handgunning itself. All of the magnums are over-penetrative, create immense muzzle flash and blast, seldom produce the impressive velocities they are credited with, and present the shooter with a recoil problem that is all but insurmountable in fast combat work. As hunting weapons, the magnums are superb, but as fighting arms they possess characteristics that cause them to be no more effective as manstoppers than the venerable .44 Special, .45 ACP, *et al*, while presenting the shooter with many more problems of controllability and over-penetration.

5

Jeff Cooper, shown here lecturing students during a class at his training facility in Arizona, pioneered early efforts towards effective handgun use in combat.

State of the art at this time remains the same, with no quantum leaps in handgunning technology having surfaced in the last decade or two. It is suspected by more personnel than this writer that the field may indeed have gone as far as it can go with present technological concepts. This, of course, remains to be seen, but it cannot be argued that we have come a long way and seem to be at the end of the road.

While technically illegal, dueling was a socially acceptable means of settling "gentlemen's disagreements" during the early and middle 1800's. Again, the handgun was usually selected as the better weapon for such activities.

The far-reaching achievements of Colt and Browning were several decades ahead of the place where the technologies of their day would place them and this has done much to confuse the "modern" student of arms who is reluctant to accept the fact that something designed so long ago can still be the best "tool for the job". This is not, as many apparently decided to interpret it, an indictment of the new, but a tribute to the genius and foresight of Mssrs. Colt and Browning in particular, as well as Georg Luger, Hugo Borchardt and Hiram Maxim. These men stand as examples of how the very course of history can be significantly and positively altered.

The genius himself. Samuel Colt, inventor of the first true fighting handgun, the single action revolver.

CHAPTER 2

THE PURPOSE OF
THE HANDGUN:
Much Abused and
Misunderstood

In contemporary times it has been popular in some circles to criticize the handgun as an anachronism — a relic from the violent past. Liberal political elements have long sought to eliminate its very existence, obviously for their own reasons, but citing the above profusely and vehemently. After all, we're now more "civilized" than we were before — aren't we?

Unfortunately, one glance at the daily newspaper, television, or a flip of a switch on your car radio gives one pause. Daily people are murdered during filling station robberies where only a few

dollars are realized; rapes, muggings, burglaries and other felonies are so widespread in parts of the country that they are regarded as being accepted facts of life. "Civilized" is hardly the word to describe such a social condition.

Thus, the handgun has begun to experience a rebirth of purpose and popularity in the civilian sector that had been dormant for generations. The very characteristics so loudly voiced by the anti-gun liberals have suddenly become quite desirable to those who seek a personal weapon for protective reasons. The handgun is, in comparison to other

Military personnel in the command or support role, provided they are reasonably well trained, can obtain excellent service from the defensive capability of the handgun.

small arms, light, portable, concealable, and generally satisfactory in its discharge of defensive duties, provided an adequate example of the breed in an adequate caliber is utilized.

While somewhat more difficult to operate effectively than shoulder weapons, the handgun more than equalizes this shortcoming with its previously mentioned assets. The trend is becoming so strong in various parts of the United States that many citizens have elected to carry a handgun for their own protection even if it places them in violation of existing laws. Not being a qualified attorney, but being a qualified citizen, I can understand why this situation exists, for many cities and states have chosen to pursue the path of penalizing the vast majority of honest citizens in a futile

attempt to obtain a short-term *political* solution to the *social* problems of crime and terrorism.

The old axiom of blaming the police for the current chaotic dilemma smacks, to me, of being the ultimate "cop out". Crime exists and flourishes because, contrary to the age-old proverb, crime *does* pay. And what's more, the perpetrators, now having their legal rights lucidly defined via legal precedent, rarely receive what one could term appropriate punishment when they actually *are* apprehended. We citizens do not have this luxury!

Add to this the glaring reality that if there really were enough police officers available to provide total protection to the citizenry, there would be distinctly more danger from the police than from the criminal! Not that the police are bad fellows, you understand, quite the opposite, but history has a term for such societies: totalitarianism — also known as a police state — and Americans particularly react to the term as if they had been poked by a cattle prod, and with some justification. This *is* the land of the brave and the free, is it not? What in the Spirit of 1776 causes us to meekly roll over and allow ourselves to be subjugated by any element, political, social or otherwise? Firearms expert (and excellent socio-political writer) Jeff Cooper couldn't have been more correct when he stated that "your best protector is you." It *is your* hide, you know — and your right!

The humorous anecdote that " a conservative is a liberal who has been mugged the night before" is fast becoming a grim reality across the nation and progressive politicians and police administrators would be well advised to recognize and understand this fact because the trend is clearly present and becoming more predominant all the time.

The law enforcement community has long accepted the handgun as being an instrument of their trade, and has gone to considerable length, not always successfully, to define its role in police operations. The fact that police officers carry a handgun on their person, either openly or in a concealed condition, does not in any way mean that they use it for offensive purposes. Since the time when the cavalry ceased to be an effective military weapon and the horses were superceded by the automobile as our primary instrument of transportation, the handgun's mission has been totally *defensive*. The fact that police often intentionally "go in harm's way" does not alter matters. They only actually *use* their handguns in their own defense or in the defense of other officers or citizens. Even SWAT teams who utilize the handgun as their primary weapon retain this mission, even

In the civilian or law enforcement mode, the handgun in its good examples can give an instantly available defensive capability against unforeseen attack. With the increase in criminal and political terrorism currently being experienced, the handgun's popularity is expected to increase dramatically.

though sometimes it is easy to forget the fact when one sees them executing building entries against an armed felon on the ten o'clock news!

The military has probably used the handgun longer than any other type of organization and yet, particularly of late, appears to understand it the least. Once the champions of weaponcraft, current military analysts have arbitrarily decided that the handgun is relatively worthless on the battlefield and relegated it to the status of being almost a military curiosity. Granted, nuclear weapons, sophisticated aircraft and artillery, and chemical and biological elements have significantly altered the course of warfare. But all these weapons have one thing in common: *they are operated by men.* And, when primary weapons fail for one reason or other those very men require a weapon for their own personal defense. That weapon must be light enough, small enough to be easily carried during the course of normal discharge of duties, and potent enough to allow the operator a reasonable chance of incapacitating a close-range assailant with minimum shots fired. The handgun fulfills this role better than any other firearm in existence just as much today as it did 50 years ago. Thus, the common statement that "pistols don't win battles" isn't quite as true as it at first sounds. Pistols do — and have — saved the lives of *men*, and men are the ones who win battles, whether they be the lowly rifleman or a division commander.

This revelation is the reason for the tremendous popularity of the handgun in any war zone, and is why men will even *buy their own* if they cannot obtain an issued one. The fact of the matter is that wearing a handgun provides the wearer with a sense of increased security, thus he is more relaxed and discharges his normal duties in a superior fashion to how he would were he not so mentally secure. This, if no other reason were valid, is sufficient to justify the existence of the pistol as a military weapon.

Generally speaking, personnel who do not require an offensive weapon . . . a rifle, submachine gun, shotgun, etc., should be armed with a handgun. Commanders, radio operators, pilots, vehicle drivers, tank crews, aircraft crews and crew-served weapon team members all satisfactorily fulfill this requirement. A commander's job is to be directing troops, reconnoitering the situation, working with maps and radios, and directing artillery fire and support, not be *shooting* at the enemy with an individual weapon, unless the tactical situation has so deteriorated that personnel shortages or his own situation demands it. Much the same may be said of the other types of personnel listed.

It has been said that the handgun's only purpose is to kill people. An objective look at the weapon and its history will show that this is untrue. Quite the contrary, in fact. The handgun's primary purpose is to *save* lives, *not* take them. It accomplishes this function by providing its wearer with the means to react to an unforeseen attack and incapacitate the attacker with minimum danger being presented to the intended victim. If the incapacitating wound also kills, then so be it, but this should not be taken out of perspective. So we can, without danger of being contradicted, say that the handgun saves lives by *stopping* unexpected assault perpetuated by someone else. There is certainly nothing evil or anti-social about this, so far as I am able to determine. People are generally nice folks, and it is unfortunate that the heathens sport the same appearance as do the honest citizens. It would be nice to proclaim that the sociological situation

For many specialized functions, the handgun is unexcelled. It is clearly easier to utilize the handgun when tight spaces are a problem, or a gas mask is worn, or when special operations require a combination of things, such as elimination of a sentry, etc.

Crew-served weapon team members require a handgun for their own defense should their team weapon become inoperable.

in America, and throughout the world for that matter, was such that none of us needed to protect ourselves against aggression. Sadly, this is simply untrue — we must protect ourselves because we have a responsibility to do so, whether we like it or not!

Historically, the turning point for the handgun came with Samuel Colt's repeating handgun: the revolver. It was only then that the handgun moved technologically ahead of edged or blunt weapons such as the sword and lance. The advent of smokeless gunpowder just before the turn of the century accelerated this superiority and there is little question that, even though the knife can still be a useful instrument under certain circumstances, the

modern self-loading pistol clearly establishes itself as the dominant force in the arena of close combat.

That the rifle also reached what can only be termed a truly modern state about the same time as the handgun in no way changes the utility of the pistol or revolver. The rifle, in contrast to the handgun, is primarily an *offensive* tool.

The coming, too, of the submachine gun in 1917 changed nothing and, although a number of authorities in the small arms field insist that a good man with a pistol can do anything a good man with a submachine gun can do, I must disagree on the basis of both extensive personal experience in this particular area and no small amount of experimentation and discussion with other qualified personnel. In my opinion, the SMG and handgun compliment each other. They do not *compete* with each other. To elaborate further would be far outside the scope of this writing so the matter will be laid to rest at this point.

In summary, the handgun remains an extremely useful defensive instrument in its adequate examples and calibers, provided it is utilized with reasonable skill and used within its limitations. That we as a culture have achieved an astounding degree of sophistication in many other fields bears no significant degree of influence upon that usefulness, liberal anti-gunners' tirades to the contrary.

Crew members of vehicles also need the handgun for their defense in the event that they must abandon their vehicle and fend for themselves.

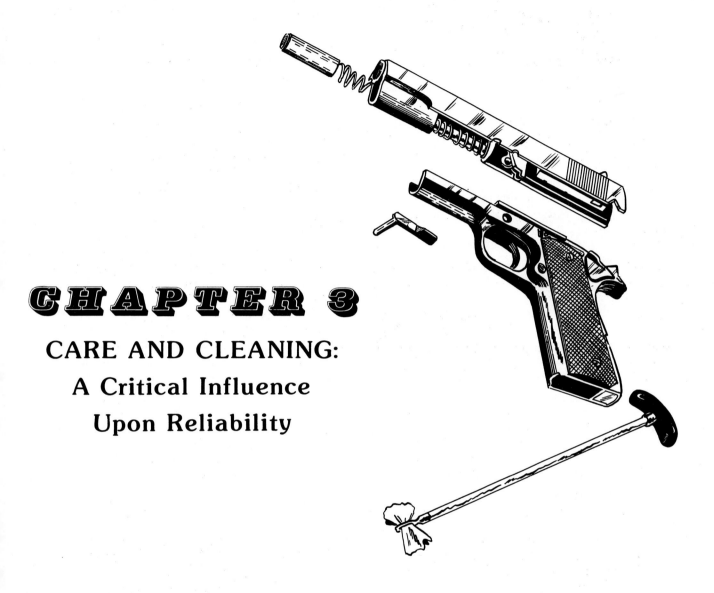

CHAPTER 3

CARE AND CLEANING:
A Critical Influence
Upon Reliability

A critically important requirement of the combat handgun is that it be *reliable*. While it would be folly to argue that the accuracy capability and stopping power of the arm are not also important, I feel that, contrary to Cooper's brilliant dictum on *"Diligentia, Vis, Celeritas* — Accuracy, Power, Speed"*, the reliability of the weapon is even more crucial, yet is almost always either taken for granted or ignored completely.

That a given handgun is powerful and/or accurate is little comfort if it does not function. Accuracy itself is given a position of importance

far out of context because any decently manufactured handgun is, right out of the box, capable of much more accuracy than all but the Master shot can efficiently utilize or even *need* in a combat situation. Super-accurate handguns certainly have a place in the overall scope of things but the field of battle isn't that place. The minimal tolerances of working parts required to obtain that tack-driving accuracy also reduce space for grit and other foreign matter to accumulate in, thus commensurately reducing its service reliability. When you experience a malfunction during a target match all

Properly cleaned and maintained, a good quality gun such as the Colt M1911 will prove reliable when the chips are down.

you have to do is raise your hand and proclaim "alibi!" When the string is over you will be allowed to clear the stoppage and complete the exercise. Any such occurrence during a handgun fight gains you only the honor of being killed by your opponent! Placed in its proper perspective, the matter stands on its own merit and requires no further elucidation.

In order to achieve and maintain a reasonable modicum of reliability, a service handgun must be periodically inspected, cleaned and lubricated. Frequency of execution of this chore is based upon two criteria: 1) Under what conditions is the gun carried and with what kind of ammunition is it utilized? and, 2) How many rounds of that ammunition do you consume in a given period of time with that weapon?

First, the conditions under which the arm is carried include not only the general *field* conditions of temperature & humidity but the method of carry, *i.e.*, open carry, concealed under a coat or jacket, waistband carry, under the arm carry, *et al* as well, because these all have considerable influence upon the effect of the elements upon the weapon. As is apparent to the more experienced student of the defensive handgun, the piece is *carried* all the time, but usually *fired* very little, at least in terms of actual defensive employment. For this reason, the weapon should be inspected every few days for general cleanliness and serviceability and maintained as required on that basis. In other words, the inspection and cleaning of your defensive sidearm isn't based unequivocally upon how often you shoot it.

What kind of ammunition you use in your handgun has considerable effect on the frequency of cleaning and inspection performed upon it. Jacketed bullets produce much less fouling in the barrel than do lead bullets. Likewise, residue and ash in the chambers, on the recoil shield, in the forcing cone and on the inside of the frame and working parts builds up more quickly from the use of handloaded ammunition than it does with factory types.

I do not recommend carrying handloaded ammunition for life and death duties because, as far as I am concerned, handloads are never quite as reliable in functioning as good factory fodder, and I want to stack the deck in *my* favor as much as possible! With current economics, however, the cost of factory ammunition is prohibitively high for practice due to the sheer quantities involved. Handloaded ammunition fulfills this particular niche well. Just remember that poor ammunition causes more fouling than does the higher quality ammo, and causes it more quickly.

Naturally, the more ammunition you expend through your weapon, the more quickly it will foul to the point where reliability is affected. This particular aspect of cause and effect is readily understood by anyone of reasonable intelligence so we will pursue it no further.

The elements of nature have a great deal of effect upon any machine exposed to them and guns are no exception to the rule. If your handgun is carried in a dry, dusty environment, inspection is just as important as it would be in a hot, humid

Extremely important, but most often overlooked during cleaning and inspection of weapon is the ammunition carried in it. Ammo with severe scratches and burrs should be removed from duty status and replaced with fresh cartridges.

Care & Maintenance Of Autoloaders

FIELD STRIPPING THE COLT M1911 AND SIMILAR MODELS

1. After insuring that the weapon is unloaded, depress the recoil spring plunger and turn the muzzle bushing clockwise.

4. Slide may now be removed from the frame.

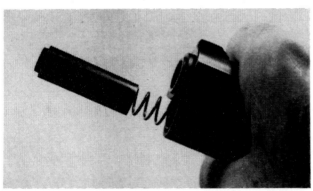

2. With the left hand, slowly ease the plunger out of the slide. Care should be taken to keep the face and eyes away from the potential path of the plunger in the event the hand should slip, allowing the recoil spring to launch the plunger skyward.

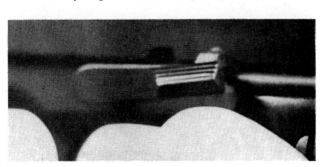

3. Takedown notch is aligned with the slide stop pin, and the pin pressed out from right to left. This releases the slide from the frame and barrel.

5. The barrel bushing is turned counterclockwise and removed. The barrel is now free to be withdrawn from the slide.

Magazines should be periodically inspected for dents, bent feed lips, and general cleanliness to insure maximum reliability.

Particular care should be taken to ascertain that grit is removed from the face of the ejector on any auto pistol. Failure to adhere to this causes many failures to eject spent cases.

The magazine follower should be inspected to insure that it functions smoothly and trips the slide stop of the gun to lock the slide back after the last shot.

Foreign matter often accumulates in the grooves in the mainspring housing and any area where checkering is located. Such matter is easily removed with a small brush.

The feed ramp area of most auto pistols should be thoroughly cleaned to remove all fouling. A clean feed ramp is essential for reliable functioning.

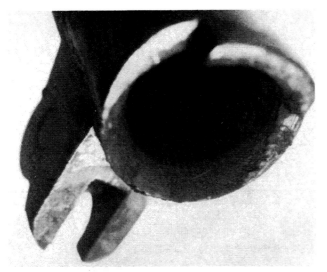

Area around chamber mouth and rear of barrel lug (bottom) also foul heavily and should be cleaned.

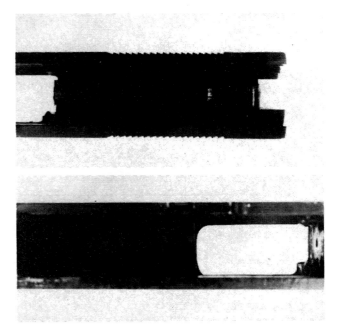

All interior surfaces of the slide should be well cleaned and lightly lubricated as well.

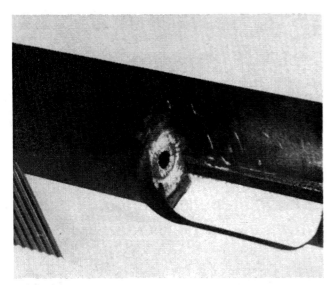

The breech face can gather a heavy accumulation of powder residue, etc., which should be completely cleaned off each time the weapon is field stripped.

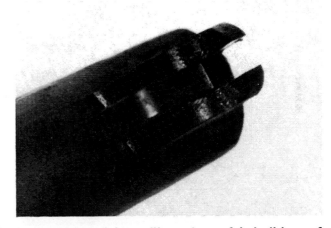

Front of barrel lug will receive a fair build-up of fouling and requires periodical inspection and cleaning.

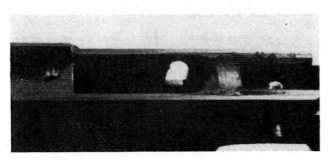

The rails on which the slide rides must be cleaned of all fouling and lightly lubricated to minimize wear and assist in reliable weapon functioning.

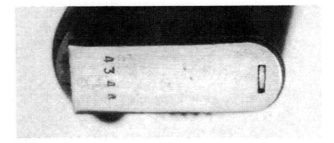

Magazines also need cleaning occasionally. If removable floorplate type is encountered, the job will be a bit easier than that experienced with the fixed floorplate styles.

Care & Maintenance Of Revolvers

Special problem areas with the revolver include the cylinder face and forcing cone area. Both receive a heavy dose of residue and powder fouling each time the weapon is fired. If residue build-up is sufficient, the cylinder will not turn, thus rendering the gun inoperative.

All grit should be removed from the bolt cuts on the cylinder to maintain proper timing and rotation.

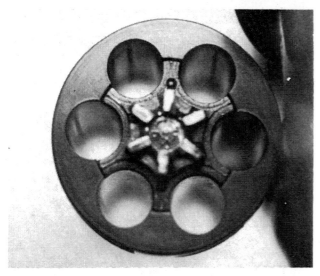

Rear of cylinder face and ratchet must be kept clean to assure proper cylinder rotation and lockup.

Bolt and interior areas of frame should be wiped clean of foreign matter and lightly lubed.

A common cause of revolver malfunction is the accumulation of grit or residue underneath the ratchet. Careful inspection and cleaning of this area will preclude such dangerous stoppages.

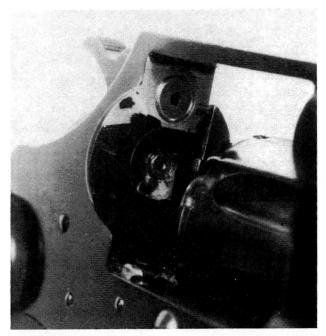

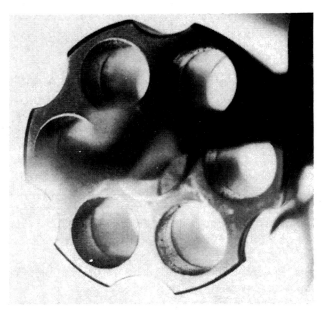

The recoil face of any revolver should be wiped clean and periodically inspected for burrs, etc. The rear of each cartridge in the cylinder must drag across this surface and any burr or piece of grit is a source of potential stoppage.

Particularly when .38 Specials or .44 Specials are used in a .357 or .44 Magnum revolver, severe fouling is experienced in the forward areas of the chambers just short of the chamber throats. If these are not cleaned, build-up of foreign matter will quickly prevent chambering of the longer Magnum cartridges.

climate. The difference is that the actual maintenance procedures in the two radically opposite environments are a bit different. In a dry, dusty area, rust and corrosion aren't your worry, so a minimum of lubricant/preservative is applied to reduce the accumulation of attracted dust particles that stick to such material. On the other hand, a hot, humid climate requires maximum protection of metal surfaces from rust and corrosion, thus a maximum of cleaner/lubricant/preservative would be applied.

If you have chosen a revolver as your defensive sidearm you must, of course, check the bore and chambers of your piece for accumulations of dust, lint, or firing residue, and remove with a brass or stainless steel bristle brush liberally doused with cleaner/preservative, followed by several cotton patches, at first soaked with cleaner/preservative, and then left untreated. *Hoppe's No. 9* or *Outer's Gun Cleaning Solvent* work well, but recently excellent all-purpose cleaners/preservatives such as *Tri-Flon* and *Break-Free* have appeared on the market. *Break-Free* exceeds U.S. Army specs by 400% and is my own personal choice for an all-in-one maintenance material.

Other areas of particular concern with a revolver are the *ratchet, extractor grooves*, the area

on the rear of the cylinder directly *beneath the extractor star*, the *face of the recoil shield, the advancing hand, ejector rod* and *bolt cuts* on the cylinder exterior.

An accumulation of any form of residue in any of the above areas can easily render your gun inoperative. When foreign matter is detected it should be carefully removed and replaced with a very light coat of lubricant. Excessive lube is as detrimental to reliable functioning as is no lube at all. In fact, in dusty areas, it is more detrimental because it attracts and traps abrasive dust particles.

Removing the sideplate from your revolver and tinkering with its internal parts is best left to only the highly experienced handgunner or an armorer/gunsmith, for the revolver mechanism is a bit fragile and can easily be damaged by the unknowing amateur. Usually the piece will not require detail stripping anyway unless it is being carried in an extremely hostile environment and/or being actually fired a great deal.

The self-loading (or "automatic") pistol is subject to the same general criteria as the revolver. Although the procedures for stripping and cleaning the auto are a bit different, it, too, will succumb to the same gremlins. Certainly no one who knows firearms will attempt to argue the superiority of the more fragile revolver over the auto with any hope of success, but even the tougher self-loader can be made to cease functioning through lack of care.

The auto by virtue of its method of operation (usually short recoil or blow-back) is prone to accumulating more fouling than is the revolver. To offset this tendency, auto pistol designs incorporate larger tolerances within the mechanism to provide room for fouling to build up without interfering with the actual functioning cycle of the mechanism itself. When those tolerances become filled with fouling, subsequent accumulations have no place to go and thus begins to hinder proper cycling of the action. Although any good auto is remarkably reliable it is a machine designed and built by men, just like any other, and is therefore fallible. We must not lose sight of this important fact.

Special areas to watch with your auto include the *locking cams* on top of the barrel forward of the chamber and their *corresponding recesses* inside the top of the slide, the *extractor*, the *ejector*, the *rails* along the frame on which the slide reciprocates, the *lug* underneath the barrel in which the link is located, the *disconnector*, and *feed ramp*.

Visual inspection of these areas is quickly accomplished and requires no special knowledge other than the basic nomenclature of the weapon and cleaning/lubrication is easily facilitated upon detection. The chamber and bore are cleaned as previously described.

The term "lightly lubricated" connotes only enough lube to be felt vaguely by touch. Exceeding that point will result in waste of lubricant material, possible loss of functioning reliability, and a minor annoyance in the form of stained clothing and constantly dirty hands.

Lubrication/preservative should be applied to the outside surface of the barrel, the bushing, the rails/grooves, the disconnector, slide stop pin and link, cam recesses and recoil lug. A very light coat of the same is allowable on exterior surfaces and, in humid climates, even advisable.

Careful maintenance of your defensive handgun will insure that it will perform to its maximum potential when the chips are down. Don't relegate this important chore to the status of being a low priority item.

It could cost you your life . . .

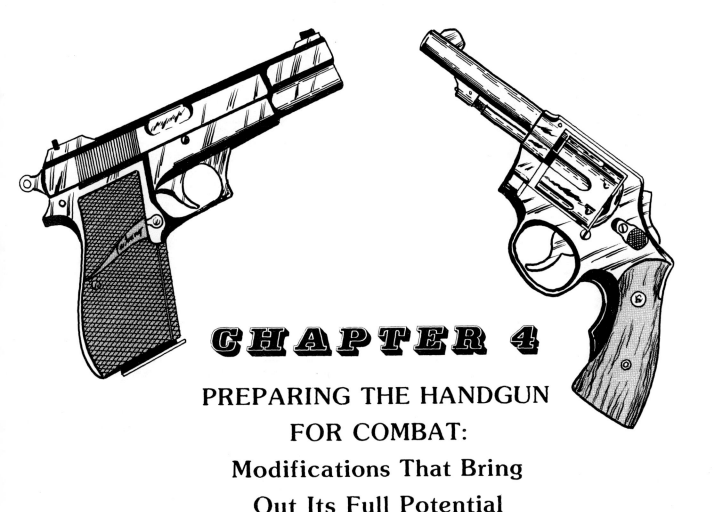

CHAPTER 4

PREPARING THE HANDGUN
FOR COMBAT:
Modifications That Bring
Out Its Full Potential

Like most machines, the majority of handguns are at least adequate for the purpose for which they were initially designed. But, still, a number of things can be done to especially equip them for defensive duty and enhance significantly their capabilities. On the other hand, many of the so-called "combat modifications" presently being advertised do little or no good whatsoever. Some, in fact, are downright dangerous.

Let's delve into this complex issue objectively and realistically. Regardless of whether your choice is the revolver or self-loader, there are only two (2) things that you *must* have to obtain maximum combat performance from either arm, aside from a high quality weapon and reasonable skill in its use: *You must have sights that are large enough to be seen quickly under time pressure and stress, and you must also have a good crisp trigger with a reasonable weight of pull.* These two criteria apply universally to either the "wheelie" or auto pistol although there are a number of specific modifications which apply solely to each weapon type alone.

Most good quality handguns are adequate for their intended purpose right out of the box. However, a few minor modifications can improve their performance and their owners' chances of staying alive.

Beginning with the revolver, note that most modern commercially made examples come right out of the box with fairly decent sights, some even adjustable. In addition, adequate triggers are the norm rather than the exception.

Trigger pull is not defined as the specific weight in pounds required to cause discharge of the gun, but, within reasonable poundage limits, a *crisp* trigger, like a glass rod being snapped, is just the ticket. Any crisp trigger with a 3-5 lb. pull weight is great for the SA auto, while more weight, say 10 lbs., is considered satisfactory for the DA auto or revolver.

Many finishes are available to the prospective combat handgunner. The most prolific and perhaps most aesthetically attractive is a rich deep blue. Unfortunately, blue, being a form of controlled oxidation itself, is little protection against rust and no protection at all against wear.

Since only the double-action revolver (DA) can be considered to be a serious defensive mechanism of choice, trigger specs apply to the DA mode of operation. The old single-action (SA) revolver is a relic of nostalgic times and must be relegated to recreational status. Anyone who has ever had to reload such a weapon under stress or in the dark, or had to engage multiple targets with the old "six-gun" well knows what I am talking about!

To reduce glare, many combat shooters have their guns bead-blasted, then blued. The result is a flat black appearance that wears longer than polished blue finishes. Sadly, it still does nothing to protect the gun from rust and corrosion, both serious problems in certain climates.

The military solution to the age-old problem of glare, rust and corrosion is to Parkerize their weapons. Boiling the disassembled gun in a controlled phosphate solution produces a coating that is flat black to a sort of poisonous green color, depending upon the needs of the weapon owner. Finish is also fairly resistant to moisture and wear except in the most hostile of natural environments. It is an excellent choice for general duty usage, and is cost-effective.

The SA revolver was the greatest thing since sliced bread in 1873, but a couple of very important things, notably the DA revolver and self-loading pistol, have happened since then!

The thumb cocking (SA) mode of operation as applied to the DA revolver is entirely too slow for application in combat and while it is understood that some authorities disagree with this statement, even superficial perusal of the techniques used by the "big boys" in the field should lay the matter to rest once and for all. Trigger cocking (DA) it is!

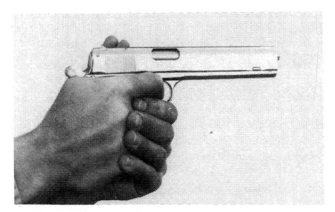

Bright chrome or nickel plating is a poor choice for a weapon intended for combative employment. Finish is too shiny to remain innocuous and too soft to resist serious handling for a sustained period of time, resulting in flaking and peeling.

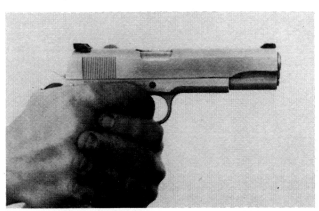

A far better choice for use in the more severe environments is industrial hard-chrome, Electroless nickel, Armoloy, Metalife and the like. Being extremely hard materials, they resist wear and tear as well as corrosion very well.

The *finish* you select for your handgun is important, for that finish will have significant effect on the service life of the arm. Most guns come from the factory with a standard blued finish which is quite pleasant aesthetically. Unfortunately,

it is no protection at all against either wear or corrosion (blueing being a slightly modified form of rust itself). A few practice draws from the holster will quickly illustrate the problem, with the blue disappearing from the muzzle and cylinder crown almost immediately. So why do gun manufacturers furnish their guns with such a finish? Because the extreme vulnerability of unfinished, or "in the white", steel to oxidation (rust) dictates that they must put some kind of finish on the gun . . . and blue is the cheapest and/or the easiest to apply, that's why. Gun manufacturers are in business to make a profit and blue is the most cost-efficient method of producing a finished product that will appeal to the prospective buyer's eye.

Add to this the problem of humidity, skin chemical composition (many defensive handguns are carried either in contact with or close to the skin), and other external environmental elements and the problem becomes quite clearly identified.

Another common finish of modern times is Teflon. This example sports a Teflon coated slide and a hard-chromed frame for maximum resistance to wear on moving parts as well as protection from nature. Author's criticism of Teflon is that it wears off too quickly for his needs.

There are a number of industrial finishes, such as hard-chrome, Armoloy, Metalife, Metalloy, Electroless nickel, and satin or brushed nickel, that greatly reduce or, for all practical intents and purposes, eliminate serious wear and/or corrosion from consideration. Hard chrome, Armoloy and Metalife are based upon chrome as their primary ingredient while nickel is utilized for Electroless nickel and brushed or satin (bead blasted) applications. All finishes of this type share a silvery appearance — the chrome base types showing a slight bluish tinge, the nickel based ones a straw or golden hue.

Whichever of these finishes the prospective combat handgunner selects is largely a matter of personal preference for all of them protect the weapon well. Personally, I find standard brushed or satin nickel a bit soft for my needs and Electroless nickel too slick to the touch to have applied to outside surfaces. It is also easily discolored by skin chemicals. On the other hand, hard-chrome, Armoloy and Metalife have worked quite well for my needs and are, therefore, my preference if plating treatments are used.

All of these finishes share one major drawback: they are all "white". To me, a light colored gun is a liability although I readily admit that, to some, it could conceivably be an asset in some situations. Thus, this particular ramification is also a matter of personal requirement based upon, I hope, a careful analysis of one's needs and consideration of the environment in which the wearer must operate.

The military solution to the problem is *Parkerizing*, which entails boiling the disassembled gun in a phosphate solution. The result, depending upon the degree of preparation and attention to applying the process itself, is a fairly hard, flat textured finish, ranging from a poisonous green, through a charcoal gray, to a rich flat black appearance (this is my own preference). Parkerizing really does resist rust and wears satisfactorily in all but the most hostile of natural environs and is normally less costly than even a marginal blueing job. I also prefer its dark appearance, as opposed to the

lighter, more easily detected chrome/nickel based finishes, even though it is not as resistant to the elements. I feel that a reasonable amount of maintenance on my weapons offsets this.

Auto pistols typically come from the factory with very poor sights of the military variety and atrocious triggers. Happily, this malady can easily and economically be rectified. Myriads of sights of the adjustable and fixed type abound in the commercial marketplace, and the number of competent pistolsmiths who will work on autos has increased tenfold in the last several years. The result is that one can now have good sight and trigger work performed on his auto pistol with a minimum of hassle and time spent waiting for the return of his gun.

A good trigger pull for an auto is about 3-5 pounds and crisp. The DA mode of operation of the revolver dictates a somewhat heavier pull of about 10 lbs.

As far as sights are concerned, the selection of adjustable versus fixed sights should be based upon the degree of flexibility desired by the weapon's owner. If you like to play around with different loads, etc., then the adjustable variety is the answer. The negative side of the issue is that their inherent fragility derived from smaller and more complex parts is much greater than that of any fixed design. I use standard service loads in all my defensive

A myriad of stocks are available to the handgunner of modern times. With each possessing positive and negative points, let us examine them. First, plastic stocks are economical, reasonably eye-pleasing, wear well, but become quite slippery to touch when they become moist. Since most people's hands will become moist when they are under stress, the author recommends careful consideration of plastic stocks, both pro and con, before purchasing them.

handguns and thus find little need for adjustable sights. This is, however, not to say that all adjustable sights are categorically worthless. A good set of Micro or BoMar low profile adjustable sights are an asset in comparison with the standard military type sights; there is no question of that!

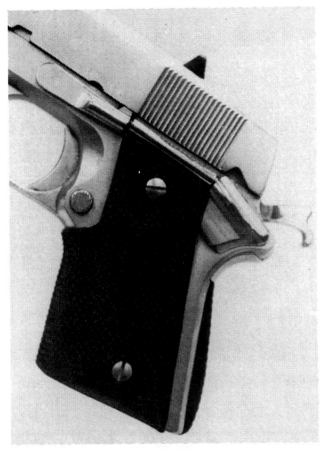

The current rage in auto pistol stocks is the rubber variety. Actual tests, however, have disclosed that these stocks hinder effective presentation of the gun from a holster by destroying the proper index of front and back strap of the gun in the firing hand.

Author feels that standard walnut stocks, either smooth or checkered, at the owner's option, provide the best index of the weapon in the firing hand. Actual timed tests have confirmed this opinion.

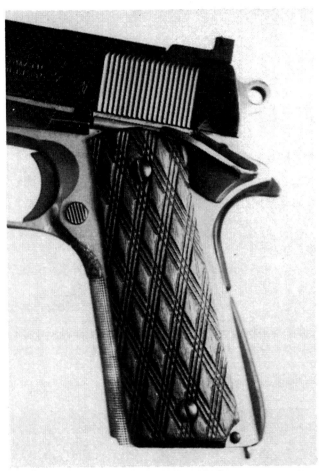

An interesting compromise between servicability and aesthetics are the "skip-line" stocks commercially available from several sources.

The topic of illuminated sights is a controversial one and many people give us different answers. I have determined to my own satisfaction that any form of colored or illuminated sights is unnecessary unless the operator of the weapon has some sort of vision disorder. At any range that one can distinguish something as actually being a target, the combination of a good Weaver Stance and regular black-on-black sights works just fine. If the light is so dim that artificial means are required then the sights appear as black silhouettes against a light target, whether they are colored or not. There is clearly no advantage to having them under these conditions either.

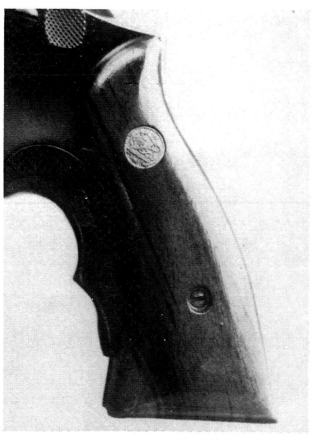

Gloss finished stocks suffer from the same maladies as do plastic stocks, but are more expensive and easier to damage. Typical finishes of this type include epoxy, lacquer and varnish.

In contrast to the detrimental effect that rubber stocks have on the grip of an auto pistol, they actually enhance the control of most revolvers. This is due to the difference in design of the two types of guns.

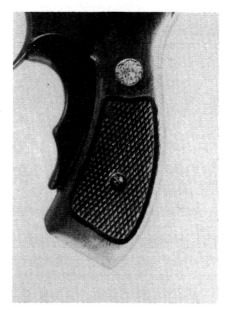

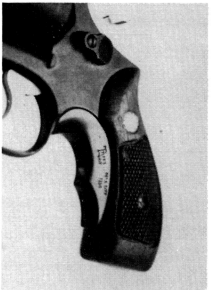

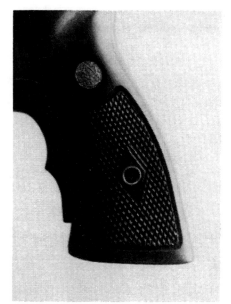

Author's choice for revolvers is simple oiled walnut, either checkered or smooth, in either square or round butt configurations, depending upon the weapon in question. The addition of a simple $5.00 grip adapter completes the combination and works magnificently.

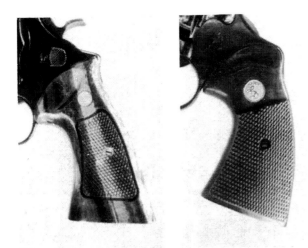

So-called "target stocks" are a deathtrap for the combat handgunner. They are large at the bottom, tapering to a smaller diameter towards the top, are too wide to allow proper index, and are finished with gloss material causing them to be quite slick to the touch. Better to avoid these at all costs!

Typical factory response to the problem of target stocks was to offer them cut away for a speed loader and call them "combat" stocks. The prospective combat handgunner should be aware of this type of maneuver and be able to properly define matters before he spends his money.

Plastic inserts for front sights are soft and quickly sustain damage that causes the sight to appear less than sharp to the shooter's eye. Also, under brighter light conditions such as found during daylight hours, quite often a good shot will inexplicably group his shots in the throat area of a silhouette target while aiming (he thinks) for the center of the chest. This is caused by the eye being attracted to the bright insert, thus at speed forcing the firer to subconsciously look for more of it. The result is an improper sight picture with the front sight riding high in the rear sight notch, causing the shots to strike higher than desired. Hmm . . . no thanks.

It is common to see target type sights installed on a factory gun instead of the proper ramp variety. A sight that has any kind of corner or hook is to be avoided.

Rear sights that are encumbered with dots, lines, or bars of color are also distracting to the eye. One must remember that you should be looking at the *front*, not the rear, sight. Anything that detracts from that relationship slows down and confuses the acquisition of a proper sight picture. With the average time frame of the handgun fight habitually hovering below three seconds one simply cannot afford this liability.

Front sight design is dictated by the requirement of allowing fast, smooth presentation of the gun to the target from any typical mode of carry, ranging from the waistband of the trousers to a $500 custom elk-lined holster. The only sight configuration that allows this is the so-called Baughman ramp. The "ramp" has no projections or corners of any kind to snag on clothing or scrape fuzz from the inside of the holster. Yet, it still offers a clear, sharp sight image at speed.

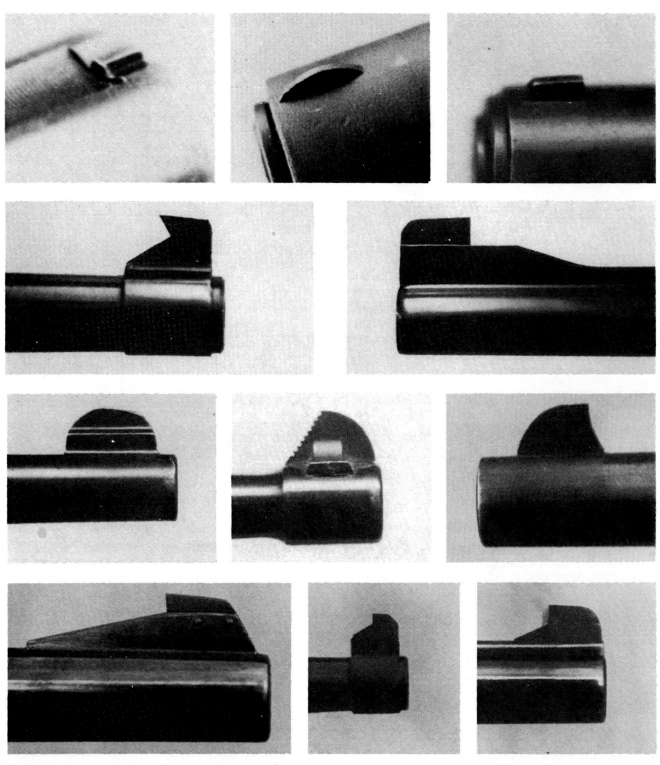

Both auto and revolver require sights that can be seen quickly at speed. However, to attain this while sacrificing practicality is a mistake. Here are typical out-of-the-box sights for both auto pistols and wheelguns. All are either too thin and low to be seen quickly under stress, or are so poorly shaped that they catch on holster, clothing and skin. Many designs of this type came from the realm of the target shooter and, while target shooting is not an evil pastime, application of target shooting accessories to a combat handgun is a dangerous activity because the two fields are only coincidentally related. Most target options are detrimental to a combat gun.

Proper front sights for the combat auto or revolver. Note absence of corners and angles to catch on

things or scrape leather fuzz from the inside of the holster.

Much the same can be said for rear sights. A wide notch provides maximum visibility and speed.

General sight configuration, however, should be kept low and simple in concept.

Standard auto pistol rear sight is too small and should be replaced with a high visibility unit as soon as possible. The same applies to corresponding

front sight blades. However, it should be understood that high visibility does NOT necessarily mean high profile (above), another disadvantage.

Adjustable sights are a nice option but not necessary for a fighting handgun. The KISS principle applies in spades when you are betting your life on the outcome. If one feels that he simply must have them, the low profile BoMar and Micro sights are the best types available at the present time.

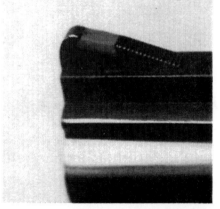

Sight inserts provide little or no advantage to the properly trained shooter under any light conditions. Author Taylor has tested all of the types currently available and finds that the only type of shooter who gains any advantage from them is the one with certain types of vision problems.

Rear sights that feature any kind of non-black appearance distract the eye from a quick sight picture and should also be bypassed when selecting sight configurations. Simple "black on black" front/rear sights, used in conjunction with proper techniques of fire, provide better potential of neutralizing targets.

To avoid chafing of skin and abrasion of clothing, edges of rear sights, as well as any other edges of the piece, should be rounded. As custom gunsmith Ikey Sparks put it, "The gun should feel like a bar of well used soap!"

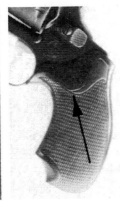

Speed loaders must clear the left hand stock panel for a quick, smooth reload. Most factory stocks must be relieved to facilitate this, but several accessory stocks come from the factory already relieved (arrow).

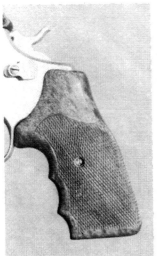

Custom stocks can do much to provide the best index of the weapon in the firing hand, but are expensive and take considerable time to build. Be careful in differentiating custom combat stocks (left) from custom TARGET stocks (right).

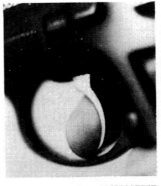
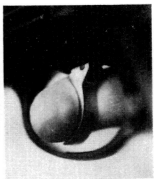
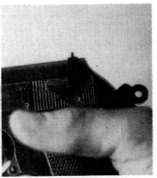

Selection of a double-action auto is a controversial issue, but author feels that having two complete mechanisms to accomplish one job is an open invitation to trouble. The DA auto provides no increase in safety and a tremendous increase in difficulty to use because of the manner in which it must be operated. While the first shot can be fired double-action, the remaining shots must be fired single-action. Thus the trigger position changes and requires a shift in the grip of the gun and the trigger finger position on the trigger itself (top). Moreover, the "hammer drop" type safeties found with such guns (center) can and often do actually FIRE the gun when manipulated. Even guns like the Czech CZ-75 (bottom) which offer either single or double-action operation cannot be as reliable as a straight single-action auto.

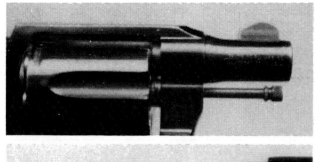

The selection of an unshrouded, semi-shrouded or fully shrouded ejector rod should be the result of careful deliberation as to the potential environment in which the weapon will be used. A bent ejector rod can indeed cause problems but the added expense of arbitrarily purchasing a gun with a shrouded rod may not be justified financially or tactically.

The fighting handgun should be devoid of any projections or sharp edges, for these abrade upon clothing and skin with negative effect. After attending a training session at which I was the Senior Instructor a few years ago Master Pistolsmith Ikey Sparks of Sports West, Inc., Denver, exclaimed: "From now on my combat handguns are going to feel like a bar of well used soap! I'm tired of bleeding from these sharp edges!" Ikey's summation of the problem is valid. Where you find an edge on your gun — remove it, even if refinishing of the gun will be required as a result. The comfort of a "dehorned" gun is a joy to behold.

Specific problem areas with the auto pistol include the collet or "finger" bushing, which should

be removed instantly upon acquisition of the gun and deposited in the nearest trash receptacle, the selection of a flat or arched mainspring housing, selection of a long or short, narrow or wide trigger, and, of course, what kind of stocks (they aren't correctly called *grips*) are best suited to your needs.

Heavy barrels aid in controlability, but may not be justified due to their increase in weight and bulk. Again, careful cogitation as to the potential use of the weapon is in order.

For those who purchase a new Colt's Mk IV, Series 70 auto, the first order of business should be to remove and discard the collet bushing and replace it with a standard GI type. Problems with the collet bushing make it a poor choice for defensive use. Target type bushings that require a wrench to remove and install suffer from the same problem as do collet bushings and should also be avoided.

The collet bushing as offered by commercial and custom sources fits the barrel too tightly and is prone to both breakage from ill-fitting and weapon malfunction from accumulation of foreign matter,

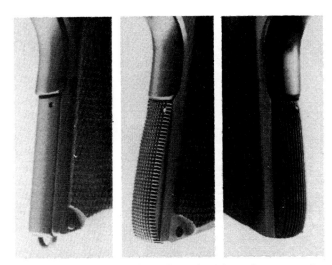

Smooth or grooved mainspring housings can be obtained at will by the interested handgunner. Even specially checkered types are offered by custom gunsmiths. The shape of your hand and simple personal preference are the primary guides to correct selection. A note of warning pertaining to checkered housings — they may abrade your clothing severely during concealed carry.

such as unburned powder. Technically the bushing is claimed to increase accuracy, which it does, but at the expense of reliability, which makes it a poor trade in my opinion. Besides, how much accuracy do we *need* for combat? And . . . do we want to sacrifice functioning reliability in exchange for an *academic* increase in accuracy? I think not. In general, if your handgun possesses enough accuracy to hit a man in the chest at 50 meters, you have more accuracy than you will ever need!

Custom "match bushings" also fall into this category for they, too, suffer from the same faults. The standard GI solid bushing should

Extended safeties are useful in enhancing the speed with which the safety can be manipulated. They can also serve as a useful platform on which to place the firing thumb for a consistent index. Be careful to remove all edges to prevent a blister, though.

Ambidextrous safeties are useful only to left-handed shooters because they have no straight left-hand safety available. The inherent weakness of such safeties makes them a poor choice unless one has no other option or is indeed left-handed.

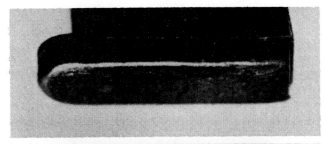

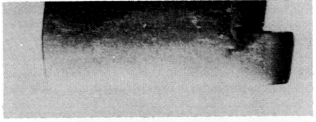

Padded magazines are useful, but often shed their pads at the strangest times! Better to be proficient with a standard magazine and not depend upon gadgetry when betting your life. Materials used for padding range from rubber, to leather, to metal, as illustrated.

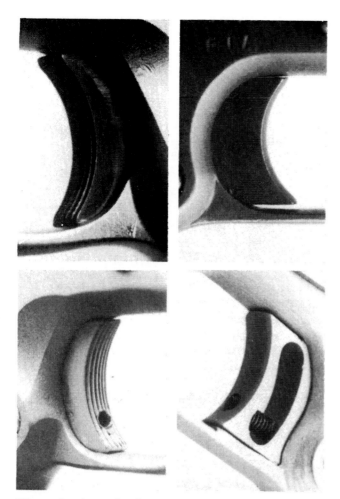

Trigger shoes on either the auto or revolver are dangerous and clumsy. Under no circumstances should one install one on his defensive handgun.

The selection of triggers for autoloaders is based upon the length of one's fingers and the size of the palm of the hand. Persons with typical sized hands and fingers should select the standard short trigger. Individuals with extraordinarily long fingers should select the longer trigger, possibly even the wider Gold Cup type. Adjustable triggers are unnecessary and often cause problems at inopportune times.

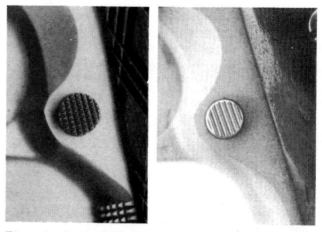

Fine checkering of the magazine release button is attractive to the eye but unnecessary for performance. The standard button works just fine!

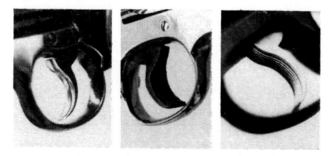

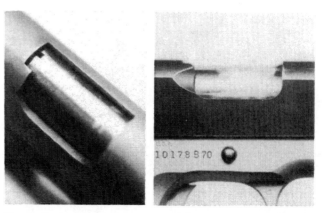

Revolver triggers should be as narrow and smooth as possible for maximum "feel" of the trigger during fast DA work. Wide "target" type triggers should be avoided and narrow grooved triggers are marginal if maximum performance is the object.

Unaltered ejection port will badly dent brass during ejection cycle. If the shooter is a serious handloader he may want to "port" or relieve his weapon's ejection port to alleviate the problem.

Bevelled magazine well is a useful modification as long as the shooter will always use that same gun. If bevelling is chosen, get a 60° rather than a 45° bevel for best results. The author prefers to stay away from bevels altogether and depend upon human performance to take up the "slack".

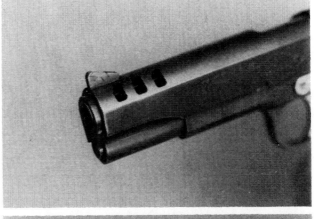

A lanyard loop is ideal for opening beer bottles in those locales where twist tops are absent. A relic from the days of the cavalry where there actually was a need to link the weapon with the horse and/ or rider, the loop does not hinder operation of the gun. On the other hand, unless one prefers it for the above-stated reasons, it is unnecessary to purchase one and have it installed on your gun.

Integral muzzle brakes, such as the KEEPER system, can assist in reducing the recoil and muzzle flip of the shorter barrelled Magnum handguns, and even does a great deal to assist in handling the big bore auto.

Stippling or checkering the front and/or backstrap of your auto does much to increase the speed with which you obtain grip index. Be careful not to have the checkering cut too coarsely, for such checkering will abrade your skin and clothing.

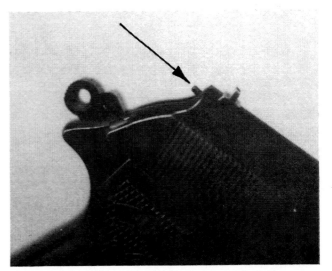

Loaded chamber indicators should not be relied upon to disclose the condition of the weapon. If you are not sure that your weapon is loaded — look!

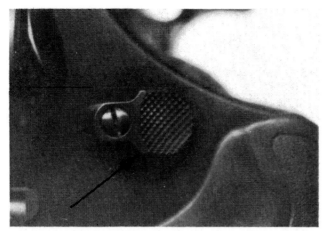

Be careful to remove the sharp edge from the bottom of the cylinder latch on your revolver. Many times that edge will cause drag on the speed loader and even cause it to "freeze" in place . . . a serious stoppage.

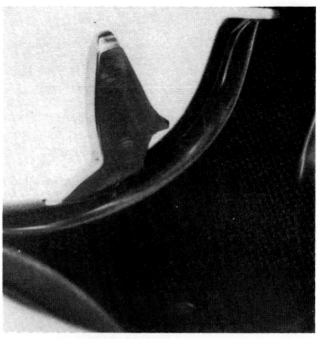

Many combat shooters remove the spur from their hammer altogether since virtually all work is done in the DA mode.

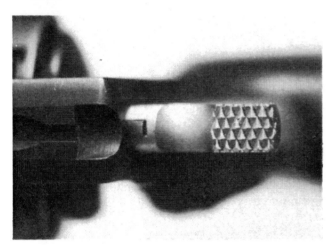

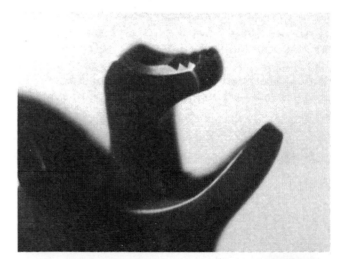

Narrow hammers are preferable to wide ones because of their lower profile. They are less likely to snag on clothing during a draw from conceal-ment. Another benefit is that guns with narrow hammers fit far more types of holsters than do guns with wide "target" hammers.

If your auto pistol hammer "bites" you in its standard configuration, you can grind a bit of it off or even replace it with a "burr" hammer.

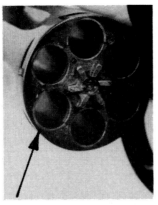

To enhance speed loading, a slight bevel can be cut into the chamber mouths of many revolvers (pointer, arrow). This "breaks" the 90° angle of the rear cylinder face and chamber and in no way harms the weapon or its operation.

instantly replace either of the aforementioned types before seriously considering the act of actually carrying your auto for defensive purposes. I feel so strongly about this point that I include disposal of either the collet or match bushing and subsequent replacement with the GI solid type along with good sights and a good trigger as being critical.

If your hands are of normal size the regular arched mainspring housing, as it comes on the commercial or military M1911A1 pistol is for you. If your fingers are not extraordinarily long, the standard short trigger that also comes from the factory is fine. On the other hand, if your hands are large the original M1911 flat housing will provide you with better index. Likewise, the man

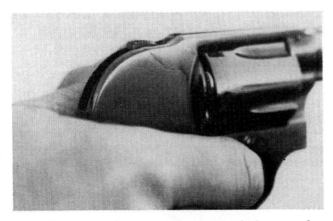

A great many shooters who carry their guns for self-defense prefer a shrouded hammer. Smith & Wesson offers several small frame .38 snubbies in this configuration from the factory while Colt provides an optional shroud for installation on your gun by a gunsmith.

with long fingers will find the long trigger more comfortable.

Wide triggers, such as found on the Gold Cup target pistol, are a hindrance for anyone and contribute nothing whatsoever towards increasing performance. The combat trigger must be "felt" any time the finger is on the trigger and the illusion of a lighter trigger pull created by the wide trigger, as well as the difficulty of fast placement of the finger on the trigger at the appropriate time during a speed draw, make it a liability.

Extended slide stops and such junk are unsafe and unnecessary for effective functioning of the weapon. Since there is no reason to shoot the auto "dry" they provide no benefit in return for their shortcomings.

It has become popular in recent years to install rubber stocks, sometimes with a wrap-around rubber panel that covers the front strap of the gun, on combat auto pistols. The idea is to enhance the grip index of the firing hand, thus providing better control and more speed. By actual timing of quite a few people ranging in skill levels from novice to Master, I discovered that such stocks actually *decrease* draw time and weapon control by as much as 4/10ths of a second. They reduce grip index enough to make the difference between life and death in a high speed situation.

The best stocks for the M1911 type pistol are the thin either lightly checkered or smooth stocks that John Browning originally designed for his gun. Like most other modern "improvements" offered for the Browning/Colt pistol, rubber stocks, target stocks and other gadgetry-oriented stocks do nothing to increase the performance of the gun and in some cases actually decrease it.

Plastic stocks or stocks with slick finishes such as lacquer or varnish are very slippery when moisture is present on them. I for one perspire a good deal when terrified and do not recommend such stocks for this reason. While this observation applies equally to either auto or revolver, the installation of rubber stocks (so hated on an auto) on a revolver is a different story. The grip angles and butt configuration of the revolver are much different than the auto and are ill-fitting in their original form. The new rubber stocks do much to correct this in a more economical fashion than do expensive, custom-fitted-to-the-firer's-hand stocks.

To increase the speed with which one may reload a revolver, a light chamfering of the chamber mouths to break the 90° corners located there is in order. Just a turn or two with a deburring tool will

Extended recoil spring guide rod is also unnecessary and prevents "pinching" the gun open to check its condition.

do the trick and make reloading about 25% easier and faster by allowing the cartridges to fall more easily into the cylinder. Unfortunately, revolvers with countersunk chamber mouths require a more complex procedure to avoid damaging the extractor star. Care and deliberation is in order during the execution of the procedure.

It should also be mentioned that one should examine the bottom edge of the cylinder release on his revolver and insure that there is no edge to catch the body of a speed loader during a fast loading maneuver. In addition, ascertain that the left stock panel is thin enough to allow adequate clearance of the speedloader itself. A stuck loader is almost impossible to clear without tools and is thus a serious liability under fire.

Trigger configurations should be narrow and smooth, with no trigger shoes or wide triggers even being considered for combat. The heart of the DA revolver is that long, smooth DA pull and wide

triggers only reduce that important "feel" of the trigger. Wide target triggers belong on the bullseye range, not in a fight!

"Speed safeties" for the auto are okay as long as the edges are removed from them, but I use them only to provide a shelf on which to place my firing thumb as opposed to giving me faster thumb safety manipulation. This way I get a better grip index and obtain it consistently at speed.

On the other hand, the ambidextrous safety, except for use by a left-handed firer, is a useless and dangerous piece of equipment. Because of the fact that there is no left-handed safety currently available, the "lefty" has no choice but to use one. But for a right-handed shooter, they have no advantage whatsoever. Think about it for just a second . . . there is no firing maneuver that you will accomplish quickly with your *weak* hand is there? Why then do you need an ambidextrous safety? The inherently weak method by which the two pieces are attached is a liability and is not offset by any tactical gain in efficiency.

Bevelling the magazine well of your auto, if done with a 60° bevel (not the conventional 45°) with no corners, will indeed enhance the speed with which you can reload. Remember, though, that the likelihood of your ever having to reload your gun that quickly is akin to being hit by lightning. Moreover, if one uses such modifications he quickly becomes dependent upon them. If you

Reshaping and polishing the feed ramp of your auto is a good idea and expands the scope of bullet types you can utilize. Bear in mind, however, that feeding reliability with exotic bullet shapes will never equal that of standard ball ammo.

then find yourself in possession of an unaltered weapon, your performance will be drastically reduced. Better to depend upon one's own skill with an unaltered gun and be that much better if he does find himself with one that features the gadgets, right?

Much the same can be said of magazine pads, which have a distressing tendency of having disappeared when you are in need of them anyway. If one is active in "practical" pistol competition, pads are useful to protect his magazines, which are perenially being dropped on the ground due to overemphasis on speed loading. But for actual combat, the old axiom of "Keep It Simple, Stupid", applies. You won't be sorry if you remember it.

The "target" hammer, offered for additional charge on revolvers, does nothing that the narrow hammer does not do equally well with reduced bulk and abrasiveness. The smaller the hammer spur the less likely it is to catch upon clothes and the finer checkering is less prone to tear skin.

While "throating" allows more flexibility of bullet design with more reliable feeding than would be experienced without it, unless one chooses to constantly use a different load and/or bullet shape (which I recommend strongly *against*), I see little need for selection of this particular option. Even a throated gun isn't as reliable with an exotic bullet shape as an unaltered gun using standard service ball ammunition. The idea that a gun will "even feed empty cases" in no way indicates that it will feed any kind of loaded cartridges. I have seen guns that would do this but wouldn't even feed ball ammo! Perspective . . . eh?

Pinning the grip safety on your auto should not be considered unless your grip style fails to depress it enough to insure satisfactory weapon functioning. If you must, then do it, but not otherwise.

Last, the selection of a "burr" versus a standard "spur" hammer should be based upon need rather than aesthetic preferences. My "carry autos" have burr hammers because the burr hammer is less likely to catch on clothing during a high speed draw out from under a jacket. This is important to me because I carry my gun concealed, but is of no value to someone who doesn't.

These are most of the modifications that are commonly encountered on today's marketplace. Remember to carefully consider *and never forget* the reason you have elected to carry a gun, the kind of environment in which you must function, and choose accessories and modifications accordingly. It is only in this manner that you can make intelligent and economically sound choices.

CHAPTER 5

HOLSTERS AND SPARE AMMUNITION CARRIERS:
Important Accessories

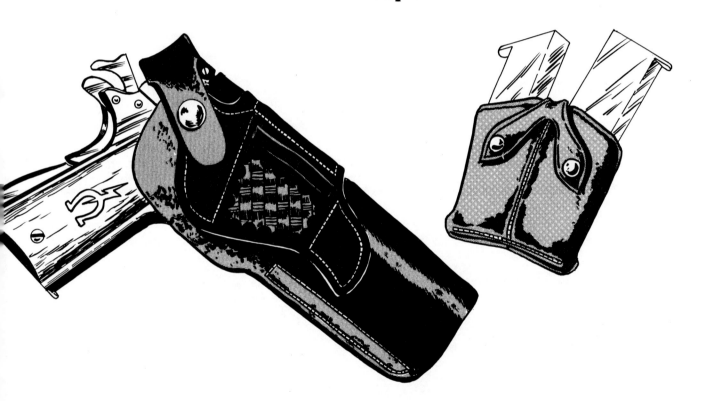

Almost as old as the handgun itself is the apparatus designed to carry it — the holster. Beginning from simple cuts in a sash draped across the chest and shoulder of its wearer, holsters have come a long way to their present state of the art.

During the late 1700's some belts were especially made to carry large handguns of that period and, as the momentous period of frontier America emerged, the holster began to take a shape more similar to that which we now recognize.

Those holsters were mostly for the purpose of simply carrying the weapon with as much comfort as possible. Remember that early Colt's service revolvers were large, cumbersome arms by today's standards. At the same time, holsters were intended to minimize the danger of loss as the wearer, usually mounted on horseback, went about his daily business.

Concealability and speed were not particularly important characteristics since the large size of the handguns of the day precluded what we would now call speed anyway. It was not until the late 1860's that much attention appears to have been given to speed of presentation of the weapon. Men

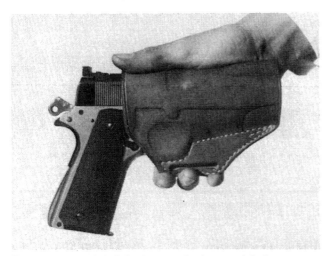

Basic auto pistol holster of the molded type as designed and produced by senior lawman and excellent holstermaker Bruce Nelson. Note that two basic requirements of a good autoloader holster are met: there is adequate clearance of the grip area and a covered trigger guard.

Milt Sparks' popular and excellent No. 1 holster is the choice of many top pistoleros such as Ross Seyfried, IPSC World Competitive Champion.

like Hickok and Earp were not known as being "fast" but as relying instead upon almost uncanny marksmanship skill and common tactical sense.

In fact, not much happened in the world of holsters or spare ammo carriers until the 1940's, when fast draw competition began to gain popularity in some sections of the United States. Competition proved to be a good experimental vehicle and various designs that increased the speed with which a handgun (usually a single-action Colt in deference to the "Wild West" that originally spawned interest in the activity in the first place) could be drawn appeared.

Gordon Wm. Davis' No. 453 "Liberty" model is probably the best general purpose holster available for the price. Both Nelson and Davis rigs can be worn cross-draw as well as on the strong side.

After about twenty years, speed competition diversified into other areas, with southern California being the hub of competitive activities under the tutelage of Jeff Cooper. When the first true "combat" matches were held in the early 1960's, many of the techniques and ideas of the old "leatherslaps" were carried over into the new field of interest.

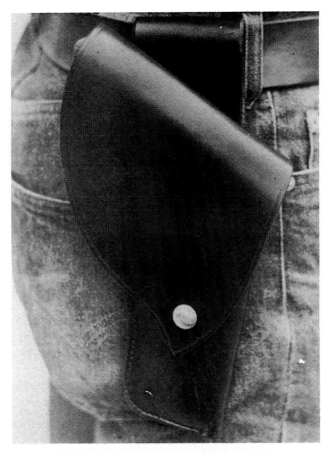

Many police departments still utilize some version of the full flap holster for either public relations or tactical reasons. Although slower to draw the weapon from than more modern designs, the flap holster does protect the gun well.

The result of these activities was the discovery of the most efficient concepts in both combat shooting techniques and in holster and related accessory design. For what continually won at the combat matches was carefully recorded by Cooper and other interested parties and, as the trends of "what worked best" emerged, various holsters and spare ammo carriers emerged in direct response.

Today there are many, many holsters available in both the factory and custom marketplace. In fact, it is safe to state that all of the basic holster concepts are well represented indeed! All combat holsters display certain universal characteristics. Naturally, high quality materials are used throughout, including even the stitching with which the leather components are sewn together. On the other hand, no more material than absolutely required is used in order to keep weight and bulk to a minimum.

We now have holsters for every conceivable purpose (and, unfortunately, some that aren't

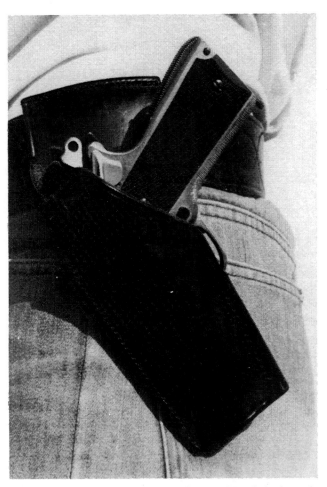

Safariland police duty type thumb break holster is available in a number of configurations. The rig shown is the most commonly encountered law enforcement auto pistol holster.

In many circles, the ankle holster is popular. This example is available from Armament Systems Products of Atlanta, GA.

The possible "wave of the future" is the plastic speed rig shown in this photo sequence. The weapon is locked in via a detent in the holster that engages the trigger guard. Gun must be rocked out through the front. The problem is that security of such a unit is marginal and the strength of the plastic tends to diminish with use, making matters worse. Verdict? Plastic technology has not yet reached a level commensurate with the design potential of the holster.

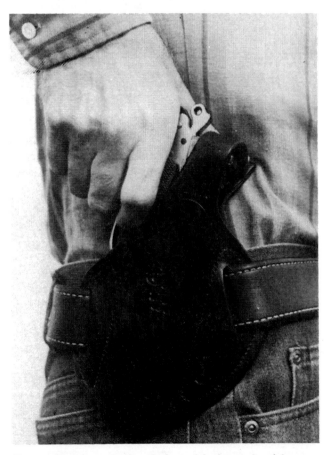

The need for maximum concealability is met with the inside the pants holster. The one on the left is from Milt Sparks. Note that instead of the dangerously insecure steel clip seen on many factory rigs (at right), Sparks' design incorporates two leather snap loops for the purpose of keeping the holster in the pants when the gun is drawn.

Example of a poorly designed holster, in this case a "pancake" type. The trigger guard is exposed, allowing the trigger finger to engage the trigger with the weapon still secured in the holster, a dangerous fault.

much good for *any* purpose, but this is a fact of all facets of modern life and should not be allowed to assume unrealistic importance). Too, there are a number of holsters that, while constructed of fine materials and exhibiting good quality workmanship, are based upon either very poor or completely invalid concepts. The prospective purchaser must continually be on the lookout for these lest he spend a sizable amount of money on inferior gear.

The "open carry" of the handgun is epitomized by the law enforcement officer's "Sam Browne" rig. Characterized by a wide (2-3") belt with either Velcro ® or standard buckle fastener, this rig must carry the weight of not only the officer's sidearm, but also a radio, nightstick, handcuffs, keys, spare ammunition and, sometimes, even a can of Mace. Since security is a prime consideration of the police officer on patrol, various ways of making the holster as "snatch proof" as possible have surfaced in recent years, particularly as the result of weapon loss sustained from surprise attack.

I do not argue that some sort of security device is appropriate but am astonished at some of the examples I see offered. Most of these designs make it so impossible to effectively draw the weapon that the wearer might as well have left it at home! Security, sure, but not at the expense of weapon availability and acquisition speed.

Happily, there exist a number of viable compromises that allow the officer, provided he maintains a reasonable degree of alertness towards his surroundings, to enjoy a good modicum of speed in presenting his piece while minimizing the danger of its loss during strenuous physical activity.

For the military man the prime prerequisites of a service holster are ruggedness and protection of the weapon since acquisition speed is not the norm on the infantry battlefield. A secondary requirement is maximum comfort to the already over-burdened individual soldier. The standard GI flap holster designed so many decades ago still protects

Milt Sparks' Yaqui Slide is a popular and widely copied belt slide design. Ideal for shopkeepers and casual wear, it is one of Milt's best sellers.

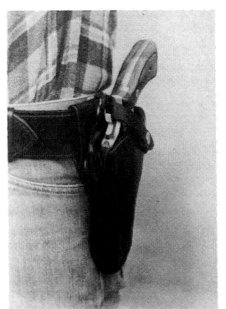
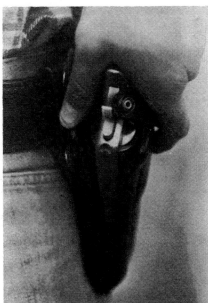

Bianchi No. 2700 front break police duty holster is shown in this sequence. It offers a good compromise between speed and security, the age-old problem of the lawman.

 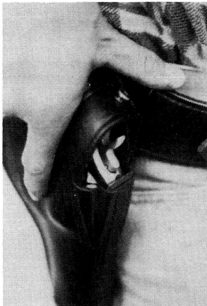 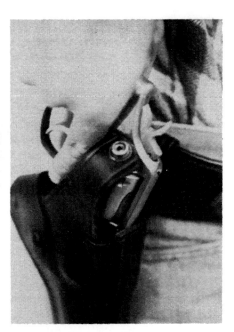

Smith & Wesson security holster. Too much emphasis on security and a complete loss of weapon acquisition speed creates a dangerous situation that should be avoided. The gun must be rocked forward before it can be withdrawn AFTER the thumb break is disengaged.

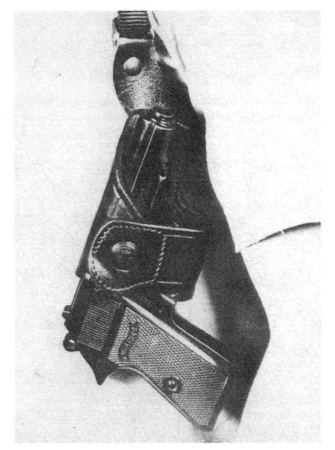

Upside down shoulder rig from Armament Systems Products shows good design and reasonable security for typical wear situation.

The Hunter field holster is adequate for hunting or recreational use, but totally unsuitable for serious combat.

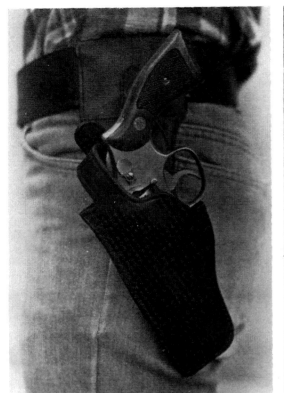 

The typical police duty swivel holster allows easier seating when the wearer is in a vehicle. Often, however, the snap that secures the holster to the shank becomes loose and allows the holster to swing freely.

the weapon well, so well, in fact, that many copies of it now exist worldwide and are used to carry virtually every type of military handgun. The U.S. M-7 shoulder holster, initially intended for use by armored vehicle crewmen, has also been extremely popular. Thus, as can readily be observed, the primary thrust of modern holster and spare ammo carrier design has been toward the civilian and plain clothes police officer.

For those who can wear them, the "inside the pants" concept offers maximum concealability potential. Even a short jacket is sufficient to hide both gun and spare ammunition, yet little if any acquisition speed is sacrificed. In fact, the only real drawback of the design is that not everyone can comfortably wear it. I, for example, am 6'1", 190 lbs., yet I cannot stand any of the inside the pants designs — they are just too uncomfortable for my particular physique.

Another item of concern here is the means by which the holster and/or spare ammunition carrier is secured to the pants belt. Most commercial designs feature a chrome plated spring steel clip, open at the bottom, that allows the holster/carrier to be inserted inside the waistband with the clip fastened around the belt. This is a poor idea and the danger of drawing the weapon *and* the holster

can best be illustrated by this humorous, but nearly fatal, anecdote:

A friend of mine is a plain clothes narcotics officer employed by a large western police department. During a drug raid on a suburban residence, he, along with several other armed officers, had occasion to enter a hallway in which a number of suspects were observed and subsequently appre-

Weak side carry allows the weapon to be drawn easily when the wearer is seated and is thus popular with many Highway Patrol organizations. Shown is the Bianchi No. 111, also a good field holster.

Assault Systems Products' updated version of the classic GI M7 shoulder rig, made from nylon and using Velcro ® instead of snaps. While of limited use for concealed carry, it is very useful for field situations where web gear, etc., is involved.

hended. In order to effectively search and handcuff these suspects, he handed his 12 gauge shotgun to one of his fellow officers, leaving himself armed with his personal Colt .45 Commander carried in a commercially manufactured inside the pants holster. In the middle of the search/handcuff procedure, a previously undetected suspect carrying his own 12 gauge shotgun emerged into the hallway from somewhere else in the house. Reacting to the warning of "Watch it — down the hallway!", shouted by a brother officer, he abruptly turned, drawing his .45 — and holster — into a near-perfect Weaver Stance. It was not until he verbally advised the suspect to "Hold it, you're under arrest — drop your weapon," that he noticed that he was unable to see his front sight, diagnosed the cause, and withdrew the holster from around his weapon and

threw it to the floor. Fortunately for him, the suspect became so amused at the humor of the situation that he put his shotgun down and proceeded to roll on the floor laughing, thus allowing himself to be taken into custody without further tensions. It isn't difficult to see how another ending, not so humorous, might easily have come to pass . . . so, if you choose an inside the pants rig, make certain that it has leather straps with snaps to retain it to the belt instead of that deadly little spring clip.

Bruce Nelson, my friend and associate, is a special agent for a large state investigative agency. Some years ago he designed a molded holster for the .45 auto that is my favorite for general concealed duty. Featuring excellent materials throughout, it fits tightly to the belt via two loops and keeps the weapon flat against the torso, thus

Old "snap-strap" type duty rig is generally adequate for typical situations, particularly of the field type, but is a good deal slower in weapon acquisition speed than a thumb break unless a disproportionate amount of practice is embarked upon.

Bianchi upside down shoulder holster. Looseness that aids in reducing shoulder holster discomfort also reduces the rigidity needed for fast weapon acquisition. This style is recommended for light duty situations or casual carry.

Milt Sparks' Sidewinder, the best shoulder rig made today — rigid, secure, yet still fast . . . and expensive, but you get what you pay for.

Jackass Leather shoulder rig features good holster design and good thumb break design but is loose and slow to withdraw the weapon from.

minimizing any telltale bulge that might disclose the wearer's armed condition. Another useful characteristic of Bruce's holster is that it can be worn either strong side or cross-draw, an increase in utility of 100%. Bruce's basic idea has been copied extensively and several other fine holster makers such as Milt Sparks, Thad Rybka and Gordon Davis all offer similar rigs. When it works — it works!

An improvement upon Bruce's idea is the No. 1145 "Realist" holster designed and manufactured by my dear friend and, in my opinion, the best of the holstermakers, Gordon William Davis. Offered with a muzzle clearance cut and friction retention unit, this holster is constructed of a steel plate sandwiched between two layers of leather to maintain its shape. To attain more speed, it holds the gun a bit further away from the torso and is thus not as concealable as Bruce's holster. But the Realist is *fast* . . . with 1 second draws and center hits on a silhouette target at 7 yards being no problem for the accomplished combat *pistolero*. Modified versions of the Realist exist that allow it to be worn cross-draw or even muzzle slightly forward. Gordon also offers a complete line of

Bianchi X2100 shoulder holster. Primarily a field unit, it is often used by plain clothes law officers as well. It allows semi-comfortable carry of even a large frame handgun and is secure and fairly fast to utilize.

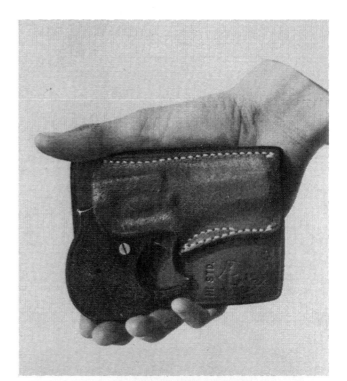

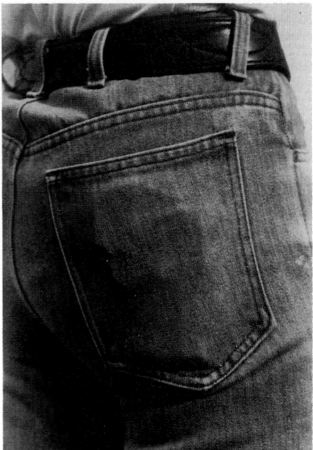

The wallet holster is the police officer's nightmare! It is an excellent way to carry a small second gun or extra-legal gun (felons only!).

belts and spare ammunition carriers that represent the absolute best available designs and quality of construction in the business.

Milt Sparks, the Grand Master of holstermakers, is also well represented with his No. 1AT holster being my favorite for general duty carry. It is a tribute to Milt's quality and character that IPSC World Champion competitive shooter Ross Seyfried uses Milt's leather gear exclusively. Ross and I have been friends for a long time and when he prefers something there is a damned good reason . . . and that's good enough for all of us!

Bianchi and Safariland offer a number of more or less standard holsters with thumb break design, as does Don Hume, who, again in my opinion, produces the best factory rigs now offered for a revolver. All models are available for auto and wheelgun alike and can be obtained easily at most of the better gun shops.

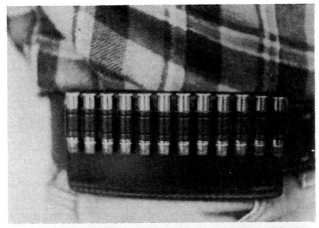

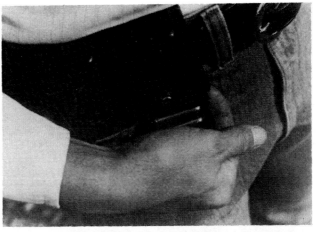

Another police favorite is the spill pouch. Although slower than a cylindrical speed loader, the pouch is flat and compact, often a choice of the over-burdened officer.

The most common police officers' accessory for many years, belt loops have fallen from favor in lieu of the speed loader. However, many good pistoleros prefer to depend upon their skill at reloading from loops instead of the gadgetry of the modern speed loader.

Casual carry of a single speed loader is easily accomplished with this unit from Accuracy Systems of Tempe, AZ.

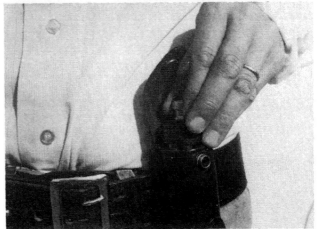

Double ended speed loader pouches open at top and bottom for less width.

Standard double speed loader pouch as offered by Safariland. Velcro® is also available in lieu of snaps from some companies.

Speed carrier for auto magazine by Rogers. Magazine can be withdrawn either upwards or broken through the front of the carrier for speed. Magazine security is marginal.

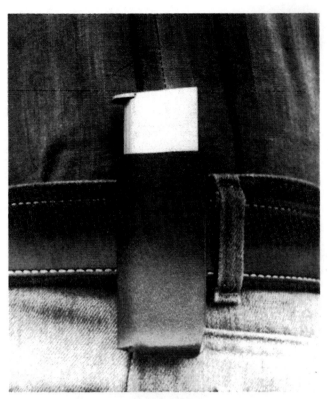

Snik (WHM Products) magazine carrier offers better security and only slightly slower speed.

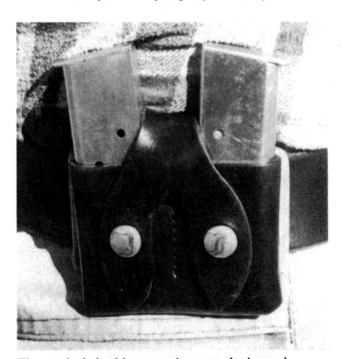

The typical double magazine pouch depends upon friction to hold magazines in place until needed. The design is generally satisfactory, but care must be taken to insure that the leather friction strap does not loosen up sufficiently to allow magazine loss.

The primary criteria of the thumb break is that the snap release *inward*, toward the torso, when actuated by the firing thumb. The tab must be, and remain so with sustained use, *rigid* with a steel shank typically employed to facilitate the task. The snap itself must be of high qualtiy, since failure to disengage at the appropriate time is likely to be terminal to the operator. Always inspect the design and quality of thumb break rigs carefully when considering their purchase.

Any auto pistol holster should cover enough of the trigger to prevent the firer from placing his index (trigger) finger inside the gun's trigger guard while the weapon is in the holster. This precludes any possible accidental discharges while the gun resides in its holster that might occur with uneducated personnel. The holster should also allow sufficient clearance for the middle finger and the third and fourth fingers to obtain a proper firing grip on the butt of the gun. The trigger finger remains extended outside the holster.

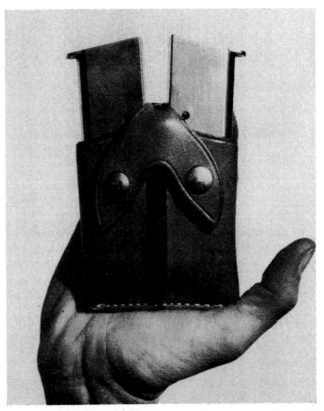

Bruce Nelson's double magazine pouch is well constructed and designed for heavy duty use.

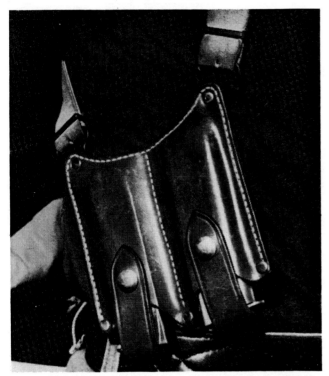

Jackass Leather magazine pouch that accompanies their shoulder holster. A simple snap arrangement holds straps that secure the magazines in place.

Old standby U.S. Army magazine pouch for M1911 .45 auto is still going strong today!

The Sparks single magazine pouch is superb for casual or concealed carry.

The Safariland speed loader is very secure against cartridge loss and fast in cartridge insertion into the gun. A plunger bears against the ratchet of the revolver cylinder and allows the cartridges to drop into the chambers.

Early speed loader — the half moon clip as used in the M1917 Smith & Wesson and Colt revolvers and the current M25-2 S&W. These are sturdy, secure and fast to use. They are still a reasonably good choice for one who carries a bigbore revolver such as the .45.

HKS speed loader uses a simple twist knob to release the cartridges. Very secure against cartridge loss and fast to use, it's the author's personal favorite.

Bianchi Speed Strip is compact and small, but not as secure as it could be.

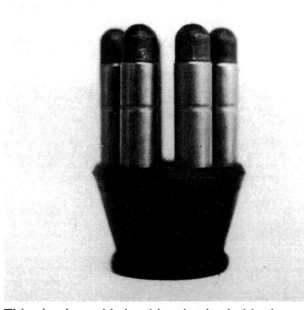

This simple molded rubber loader holds the cartridges with a small lip that folds over the cartridge rims. It is very insecure and clumsy to use.

54

Bucheimer Co. speed loader is fast and sure, but constructed of fairly brittle plastic that breaks more easily than some other materials now in use. One need only insert cartridges into the cylinder and press a button to release.

Holsters intended for the DA auto or DA revolver need not cover the trigger guard, for a long, heavy pull is required to fire the gun, in contrast to the short, light pull of the SA auto. The grip clearance, however, remains a valid requirement.

The old "Border Patrol" type holster of the 1930's is still going strong, with its long strap providing security against weapon loss. Basically a good general purpose holster design, its only disadvantage is that unless the firing hand is habitually kept below the level of the snap/strap, it is slow to manipulate.

In the last few years, "cross-draw" rigs have enjoyed increased popularity due to their use in IPSC competition (where, sadly, they are habitually worn on the abdomen instead of the point of the hip where they belong). Game playing to the contrary, a cross-draw has the advantage of being highly concealable when correctly worn, reasonably comfortable, and allows very fast weapon presentation from under a coat or jacket. An additional asset is that the gun may be easily drawn while the wearer is sitting down.

There is, of course, a place for "belly carry", but the conditions under which it is useful are so specialized that they are best left up to the reader's imagination.

With plastic becoming a front runner in the construction of almost everything these days, it is no surprise that we now also see plastic holsters and magazine carriers. The Rogers and Snik, for example, are rugged, reasonably good looking, simple and quite fast. Unfortunately they aren't secure enough for general service and the plastic used in their construction seems to lose strength with age, thus causing them to be even more

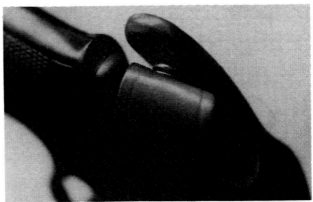

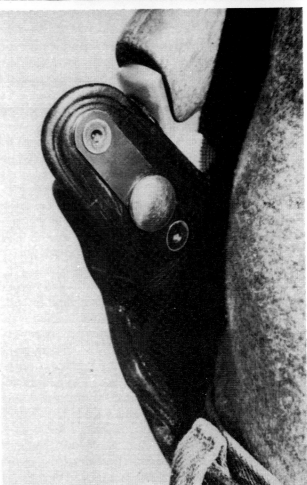

Close-up of properly designed thumb break unit. It must be rigid to allow a crisp break of the snap when actuated.

prone to weapon loss during intense physical activities. So, until technology overtakes this basically sound concept, I cannot comment favorably on any currently offered plastic rig.

The last of the conventional designs is the shoulder holster. Ultimately concealable and fast to use, all examples suffer from a common malady — due to the loss of air circulation in the wearer's clothing caused by the harness, they are uncomfortable to wear outside of a completely air-conditioned environment. Attempts to minimize this problem have resulted in a proportionate loss of utility, for the weapon *must* remain rigidly at the spot to which the firing hand is trained to move when the stimulus to draw the gun is received. If the gun has moved — you are in trouble! The more rigid the holster, the more uncomfortable it is because the straps that hold the rig tightly around the torso also bind up the wearer's clothing.

Let us now examine spare ammunition carriers. All of the major holstermakers in the country produce several basic designs of both single and double magazine carriers for use with the auto pistol. Oddly enough, all of them exhibit the same good and bad points as do their accompanying holsters, for they attach to the belt and operate in much the same way as do those holsters.

Law enforcement officers who carry arms openly usually prefer a double magazine carrier with flaps that fasten with either Velcro® or snaps for security reasons, while the more casual carry of the firearm allows more emphasis on speed.

Spare magazines may be held in the carrier by friction, magnetism or simple gravity and the specific needs of the wearer are the primary consideration when a prospective carrier is examined. Again, remember to keep it as simple as possible . . . you won't regret it.

Revolver speed loaders are most often carried in a single or double pouch of considerable bulk, and many dislike them for this reason. An acquaintance of mine claims that he has to turn sideways to get through a door when wearing one. Although he offers his criticism humorously, he does indeed have a point! Large men will unquestionably experience more binding against doors and other close objects when wearing such a pouch.

While regarded in some circles as "obsolete", belt loops, spill pouches and strip loaders are all legitimate. It is unprofessional to claim otherwise for, as previously noted, there is indeed a place for

everything. The key to success is to correctly diagnose one's needs first.

Do not forget that holsters must be mounted rigidly on the belt to eliminate or at least minimize wobble and swivelling. To facilitate this, the belt must be stoutly constructed, preferably of 14 oz. leather if possible. The subject of holsters is loudly discussed at every gathering of interested personnel, but belts are curiously ignored in spite of their importance.

Good equipment is not inexpensive, but as with everything else in this world, you get what you pay for. My recommendation is to obtain the best quality/design possible.

It will more than pay for itself in a short period of time.

The author using his personal favorite holster, the Gordon Wm. Davis No. 1145 "Realist". Author feels it is the best general-purpose, non-police holster available today.

CHAPTER 6

HANDGUN STOPPING POWER:
The Name Of The Game

In the *purpose* section of this book, we examined why the handgun primarily exists and why it has reached its present state of the art. It was said that the weapon is intended for *reactive, defensive* use. In other words, to bring to a conclusion favorable to its wearer, a combative altercation precipitated by someone else, with minimum shots fired, preferably no more than one per target.

Many terms have been coined and many theories have been perpetuated to define and explain how this mission is accomplished . . . and to compare various handgun cartridges against each

other in how they accomplish the stated task. In this chapter we will investigate the most popular ideas on this abstract and somewhat emotional subject.

As occurs with many complex subjects, *terminologies* play an important, if not critical, role. In connection with the subject of stopping power, we often hear the term "Knockdown Power" used. In the literal sense we must interpret this as defining the ability of a given cartridge to *physically sweep a man from his feet when hit by its projectile.* Simple arithmetic tells us that the term itself is

Pocket pistols, although useful in certain situations, are far too anemic in their stopping power to depend upon for general purpose employment.

suspect, for Newton's irrevocable Law of Nature applies:

"For every *action*, there is an equal, but opposite, *reaction*."

Translated to simple terms, this means that any arm that can produce sufficient force to phyiscally *knock* a man from his feet with the impact of its projectile *would also knock down the person firing the weapon that launched that projectile!*

As applied to the field of discussion, this is an over-simplification, of course, but is, for the most part, still valid. If the penetration of the projectile could be discounted, the energy (or *kinetic impact*

Exotic weapons, such as this COP, are clumsy to utilize effectively, although offered in a serious caliber.

energy, as it is properly defined) of the projectile would be the sole element in question. However, since this in no way can actually be applied, we must say that the theory of Newton's Law only approximately applies.

From a good deal of personal experience and observation, as well as no small amount of research into the subject, I find that "knockdown power" as applied to the field of combat handgunning is largely invalid. No handgun now in existence can physically produce enough energy upon projectile impact on the target to knock down that target. Thus, comparisons of energies produced by given cartridges serve only as interesting points of discussion, rather than a legitimate means of measuring those cartridges' abilities to incapacitate an assailant.

STAR Model PD, a .45 caliber "pocket pistol"of sorts, features excellent design, but spotty quality control. This is a problem to one who must depend upon the weapon to save his life.

The so-called "energy school of thought" is populated mostly by the inexperienced handgunner and the engineer, neither of whom possess sufficient experience in the field of deadly combat to express a qualified opinion on the subject.

It is interjected at this point that I am in no way attempting to harangue those who fall into these two categories. I am merely pointing out that neither jet airplanes nor bumble bees can fly, according to engineers, and the old adage about "a little knowledge being a dangerous thing, *i.e.*, the 2nd Lieutenant with a map syndrome" is worth seriously considering. The world is not a terribly complex place, but there are many things that refuse to be placed in nice, neat little boxes of explanation and stopping power is one of those things.

There are simply too many variables to consider to make blanket statements that so many foot-pounds of energy performs the task of stopping an enemy better than some other quantity of energy rendered by another cartridge. To name a few, we must consider the mental state of the adversary, his size, *i.e.*, height and weight, his nerve sensitivity, his muscle bulk and tone, water content of tissue, and where the projectile strikes him. None of these things can realistically be included into a formula because they not only vary tremendously from person to person, but they often vary daily in the same person! Case in point?

Any serious attempt to prove that energy produced by handgun cartridges has a significant bearing on *incapacitating* an adversary irrevocably crashes into the above-mentioned variables. More importantly, when results obtained from mathematical calculations of energy are compared with *actual field observations* (the acid test, is it not?), little correlation is found.

Modern entry into the bigbore service pistol category is the Heckler & Koch P9 in .45 ACP. Rugged, well designed and accurate, it is surpassed only by the venerable Colt M1911 .45 in general utility and ease of use.

Updated versions of "old ugly", the M1911 .45 auto, are still as popular as ever and the .45's reputation as a manstopper remains undiminished.

To place things in a more lucid perspective, we must state that handguns just don't produce enough kinetic energy to: a) *knock* anyone off their feet, and, b) even *incapacitate* them.

There is little question that some cartridges perform their manstopping duties in a superior fashion to others. In this case we already have an answer, but are in search of the question! As far back as handguns have been used against men it has generally been known that the larger projectiles, assuming adequate velocities for penetration into vital organs is obtained, are better "stoppers" than

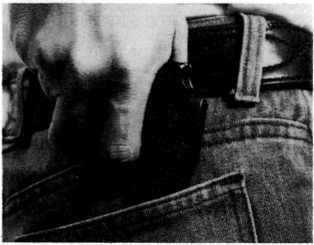

Most pocket handguns are offered only in the small calibers .22, .25, .32 or .380. All of these suffer from a lack of dependable stopping power. This is a serious consideration that cannot be ignored when weapon selection is pondered.

Beware of obsolescent guns and ammunition even though both can be obtained at bargain prices quite often. Better choices exist and should be pursued.

the smaller ones. This does not mean that the big bullet *always* succeeds or that the smaller one *always* fails either. It means that, on the general scale, the big bullet stops more frequently than does a smaller one. *They both can, and do, fail.* The smaller projectiles just fail *more often*, no more, no less.

General Julian Hatcher, Chief of Ordnance for the U.S. Army in the early part of this century, endeavored to discover why this was so. A scientist of the purest form, Hatcher was uninterested in advancing his personal status. He was interested only in attempting to find an explanation for an observed reality. It is primarily in this way that he differed from almost every other individual, even to this day, who renders an opinion on the subject.

Commissioning Col. John T. Thompson (the father of the magnificent Thompson submachine gun) and U.S. Army Surgeon General's Office representative Col. Julius A. LaGarde to perform an in-depth study into the subject, Hatcher discovered that his starting point, kinetic energy, failed to

satisfactorily correspond to observed reality. Correctly assuming that there must be some element missing, Hatcher re-reviewed the findings of Thompson and LaGarde and attempted to create a mathematical formula that would be sufficiently accurate to qualify as being at least an "educated guess" as to why the actual phenomenon of stopping power occurs. Without entering into a myriad of arithmatic terminologies that would serve only to put the reader to sleep (as well as possibly the writer!), it is safe to say that when Hatcher included projectile *mass*, as well as its weight and velocity, into his calculations, the results began to correspond remarkably well with reality.

While not attempting to claim 100% validity, Hatcher did state that, if one were to skim off the inevitable exceptions that occur at both the top and bottom of the scale, the remaining 85% of the findings were valid. This he did, and the figure of 85% accuracy obtained by Hatcher remains the best "educated guess" we have to this day.

For reference purposes, the formula for computing kinetic energy is expressed as:

$$\frac{W \times V^2}{450,240} = KE$$

W = bullet weight
V = bullet velocity

KE = kinetic energy in foot pounds

Hatcher's formula of *Relative Stopping Power* is computed thus:

$$\frac{1}{2(32.16)} \times \frac{WV}{7000} \times A \times y = RSP$$

Single action revolvers should be used only for recreational use, not combat. Their fragility, difficulty of use and lack of versatility make them a poor defensive choice.

RSP = relative stopping power
W = bullet weight in grains
V = initial velocity in feet per second
A = cross sectional area of bullet in
square inches
y = an empirical bullet shape factor
defined as follows:
Lead Round Nose: 1.0
Full Metal Jacket Round
Nose: .9
Lead Wadcutter: 1.25
Lead Semi-Wadcutter: 1.25
Lead Flat Point: 1.05

The inclusion of a bullet shape factor (coefficient) and attention paid to the composition of the projectile itself adds much to the accuracy of the computations derived from the formula. All subsequent attempts to produce a more accurate formula have met with dismal failure.

An example of such an attempt was the Law Enforcement Assistance Administration's study into what they called "Relative Incapacitation". Gelatin blocks, a computer "man", high speed photography and samplings of every major brand of commercially available handgun ammunition were used in the "tests", and the results were fed into a computer.

To say the least, the results were interesting, and the so-called preliminary report was circulated to every law enforcement agency in the United States. The "findings" disclosed in the preliminary report failed totally to correspond to reality, proving only that when one feeds garbage *into* a computer, one gets garbage *out* of a computer.

Frangible bullet technology has done much to improve many cartridges, but cannot make a powerhouse out of something that is simply not there. This should always be understood when considering calibers.

9mm Parabellum has been in use since 1908 and is offered in a fair number of configurations. Left to right: 125 gr. military ball, 124 gr. Hornady factory jacketed truncated cone, Speer 125 gr. JSP, Geco 115 gr. JSP and Remington 124 gr. JHP.

The subsequent full report contradicted the preliminary one substantially. However, it was not widely circulated for some reason. In an effort to explain the horrendous difference between reality and the results of the preliminary report, at least one firearms expert of considerable reputation advised me that he knew for a fact that the entire program was an attempt to justify the small caliber for law enforcement use, and that members of the test staff had actually admitted this in private.

Whether or not this is true, it is safe to say that many of the assumptions made by the LEAA test group were arbitrary and, to say the least, invalid. Therefore, it is certainly no surprise that when these assumptions were programmed into the computer in conjunction with the other data, the results were less than accurate. A reproduction of the "RII" table is included herein.

In 1974, Jeff Cooper published his "Short Form" of stopping power calculations in an effort to simplify Hatcher's complex method. Basically Jeff's formula was to multiply the bullet *weight* (in grains) times its *velocity* (in feet per second) times the weapon's bore sectional area (in fractions of an inch) with all figures rounded off to make mental computation easier. A sample equation appears:

Weight (150 grs.) x Velocity (1000 fps)
x Bore Sectional Area (.38 caliber = 1.0)
= 15.00

INDEX OF HANDGUN CARTRIDGES

CARTRIDGE	GRS.	BULLET STYLE	MUZZLE VELOCITY	MUZZLE ENERGY	BARREL INCHES	CARTRIDGE	GRS.	BULLET STYLE	MUZZLE VELOCITY	MUZZLE ENERGY	BARREL INCHES
.22 JET	40	SP	2100	390	8-5/8	.38 SPECIAL INTERNAT'L.	158	L	1090	414	6
.221 FIREBALL	50	SP	2650	780	10-1/2	.38 SPECIAL	200	L	730	236	6
.25 AUTO (6.35mm)	50	MC	810	73	2	.38 SPECIAL	158	MP	855	256	6
.256 WIN. MAG.	60	HP	2350	735	8-1/2	.38 SPECIAL WC	148	L	770	196	6
.30 LUGER (7.65mm)	93	MC	1220	307	4-1/2	.38 SPECIAL MATCH	148	HBWC	775	196	6
.32 SHORT COLT	80		745	100	4	.38 SPECIAL MATCH, IL	148	L	770	195	6
.32 LONG COLT, IL	82		755	104	4	.38 SPECIAL MATCH, IL	158	L	855	256	6
.32 COLT NEW POLICE	100	L	680	100	4	.38 SPECIAL HI-SPEED	158	L	1090	425	6
.32 AUTO (7.65mm)	71	MC	960	145	4	.38 SPECIAL	158	SWC, L	1050	—	6
.32 AUTO (7.65mm)	77	MC	900	162	4	.38 SPECIAL	158	RN	900	320	6
.32 S&W	88	L	680	90	3	.38 COLT NEW POLICE	150	L	680	154	4
.32 S&W LONG	98	L	705	115	4	.38 SHORT COLT	125	L	730	150	6
7.5 NAGANT	104	L	722	120	4-1/2	.38 SHORT COLT, GREASED	130	L	730	155	6
.32-20 WIN.	100	SP	1030	271	6	.38 LONG COLT	150	L	730	175	6
.32-20 WIN.	100	L	1030	271	6	.38 SUPER	107	JHP	1430	486	5
.357 MAGNUM POLICE	110	JHP/SP	1690	697	6	.38 SUPER	112	JSP	1435	504	5
.357 MAGNUM POLICE	137	JSP	1630	808	6	.38 SUPER	130	MC	1280	475	5
.357 MAGNUM	158	SP	1550	845	8-3/8	.38 AUTO	130	MC	1040	312	4-1/2
.357 MAGNUM	158	MP	1410	695	8-3/8	.380 ACP	88	JHP	1065	227	4
.357 MAGNUM	158	L	1410	696	8-3/8	.380 AUTO	95	MC	955	192	3-3/4
.357 MAGNUM	158	JSP	1450	735	8-3/8	.38-40 WIN.	180	SP	975	380	5
9mm PAR.	90	JHP	1485	441	5	.41 MAGNUM	170	JHP/JSP	1775	1188	8-3/8
9mm PAR.	112	JSP	1325	425	5	.41 REM. MAG.	210	L	1060	515	8-1/4
9mm PAR.	116	MC	1165	349	4	.41 REM. MAG.	210	SP	1500	1050	8-1/4
9mm PAR.	115	JHP	1140	330	4	.44 S&W SPECIAL	246	L	755	311	6-1/2
9mm PAR.	124	MC	1120	345	4	.44 MAGNUM	180	JHP/SP	2005	1607	6
.38 S&W	146	L	685	150	4	.44 REM. MAG.	240	SP	1470	1150	6-1/2
.38 S&W	146	L	730	172	4	.44 REM. MAG.	240	L	1470	1150	6-1/2
.38 Mk II	100	MC	620	153	5	.44-40 WIN.	200	SP	975	420	7-1/2
.38 SPECIAL POLICE	110	JHP/SP	1282	399	6	.45 COLT	250	L	860	410	5-1/2
.38 SPECIAL POLICE	125	JHP	1370	520	6	.45 COLT	255	L	860	410	5-1/2
.38 SPECIAL, IL	150	L	1060	375	6	.45 AUTO	190	JHP	1060	473	5
.38 SPECIAL, IL	150	MC	1060	375	6	.45 AUTO	230	MC	850	369	5
.38 SPECIAL INTERNAT'L.	158	SWC KK	1110	430	6	.45 ACP	230	JHP	850	370	5
.38 SPECIAL	158	JHP	1150	460	6	.45 AUTO WC	185	MC	775	245	5
.38 SPECIAL	158	L	855	256	6	.45 AUTO MC	230	MC	850	369	5
						.45 AUTO MATCH	185	MC	775	247	5
						.45 AUTO	210	L	710	235	5
						.45 AUTO RIM	230	L	810	335	5-1/2

IL — INSIDE LUBE   JSP — JACKETED SOFT POINT   JHP — JACKETED HOLLOW POINT   MP — METAL POINT
RN — ROUND NOSE   HP — HOLLOW POINT   WC — WAD CUTTER   L — LEAD
MC — METAL CASE   SP — SOFT POINT   LUB — LUBRICATED

A score of 20 is "passing" and Cooper's formula does much to ease the burden of computing comparative values between given cartridges.

It does not, however, take into consideration the ease and speed of the modern pocket calculators which allow increased speed and flexibility of computation. In an effort to recover the degree of accuracy lost in rounding figures to the nearest convenient tenth and ignoring Hatcher's bullet shape coefficient as well as taking modern expanding bullets into account, I modified Cooper's basic formula into what I feel is a somewhat more accurate formula.

The *exact* projectile weight in grains (W) is multiplied times the *exact* velocity (V) (*obtained via chronograph from real guns with service-length barrels* instead of manufacturers' published specs —

they differ radically, you know) times a Bore Sectional Area Factor. Then, if the velocity of the projectile exceeded Mach 1 (1088 fps — the accepted figure for reliable bullet upset on the average), 25% is added to the final figure. The table of my results is included for reader perusal and shows the "Taylor Modified Short Form" results of all of the standard loadings of modern handgun cartridges worth considering both if the expanding bullet actually *does* and *does not* upset.

Another interesting fact worth discussion here is that the LEAA assumptions on bullet performance were based upon their passage through gelatin, not people. I readily admit that there is a distinct shortage of human volunteers for such an endeavor, however, gelatin differs so radically from

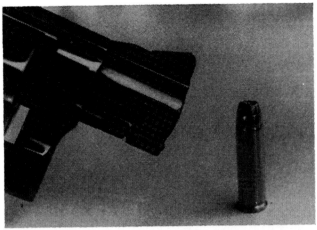

The main problem with .38 Specials is that they almost never expand out of typical service barrel lengths, ballistics tables notwithstanding. The problem is aggravated by the use of such ammunition in the ubiquitous snubby revolver.

the human structure in both composition and material that I am astonished that anyone could, with a straight face, advance results obtained from such a suspect test media.

Another important assumption on the part of the LEAA test team was that the *temporary wound cavity*, created at the instant of bullet passage through the target medium, had significant effect upon incapacitation. In reality, the *permanent wound cavity*, that is, the *actual amount of damage* done to tissue, bones and nerve endings obviously has more effect upon matters than does the temporary cavity, since the temporary cavity *collapses almost instantly from the resilient effect of the human paste.*

Yet another fallacy of the LEAA tests was the assumption that a jacketed bullet will *always* upset

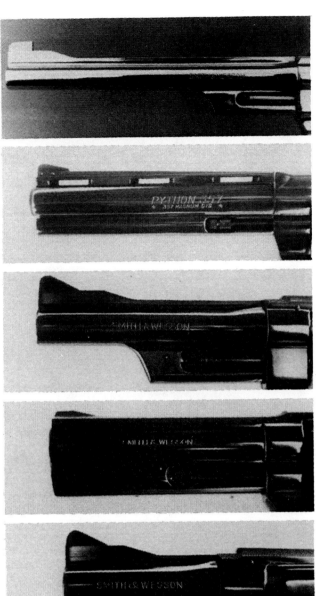

Original .357 Magnum specs were obtained from an 8-3/8" barrel. Obviously such a weapon was too ungainly for any kind of combative carry, thus barrel lengths were reduced over the years. Typical length of .357 barrels is now 4". From top to bottom, barrel lengths shown are: 8-3/8", 6", 5", 4", 3½", 3" and 2½".

.357 Magnum is not what it is cracked up to be when encountered in the typical 4" barrel. At least a 5-6" tube is needed to produce the velocity needed to make the .357 perform as it should.

How barrel length affects velocities and resultant bullet performance is illustrated above. Bullets are 110 gr. Super Vels fired from (left to right) 8-3/8" barrel, 6" barrel, 5" barrel, 4" barrel, 3" barrel and finally a 2-1/2" barrel. Bullets were fired into water-based clay for recovery purposes and should not be expected to expand in humans in the same manner as they did in the denser medium.

Danger of artificial testing mediums is illustrated by these 110 gr. .357 bullets fired from a revolver with a 4" barrel. Slug on the left was fired into clay while the bullet on the right was recovered from a felon shot during the conduct of a robbery. Both bullets were from the same box of ammunition.

.41 Police load was an excellent idea, ruined by so-called "Madison Avenue" marketing. Mid-range police load was overshadowed by the full house Magnum hunting load and resultant lack of weapon control caused severe problems for most police officers.

One of the black powder cartridges that survived the shift to smokeless powder was the .44 Special. An excellent manstopper without exotic bullets, it suffers only from the lack of a current, full size production gun chambered for it.

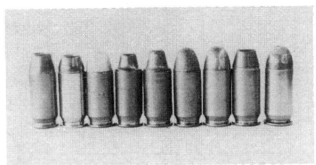

The leader in the combat field is unquestionably the .45 ACP of M1911 auto pistol fame. Now available in almost any type of configuration one might desire, the author still urges use of standard 230 gr. ball for maximum feeding reliability even in "throated" guns. From left to right are Super Vel 190 gr. JHP, new Super Vel 190 gr. JHP, Winchester 185 gr. Silvertip, Remington 185 gr. jacketed SWC, handloaded 200 gr. (H&G No. 68) lead SWC, 225 gr. lead RN handload, 230 gr. ball, 230 gr. Hornady truncated cone and Norma 230 gr. JHP.

"Dirty Harry Special" — the venerable .44 Magnum. Originally designed for the hunting of medium to large game, the .44 "Maggie" has of late been used for combative purposes as the result of its cinema exposure. It is, however, over-penetrative for combat work, too difficult to effectively control and produces excessive blast and flash.

Since the .45 is not capable of supersonic velocities virtually all attempts at bullet expansion result in failure. Shown is the Super Vel 190 gr. JHP, the most prestigious of the frangible bullet .45's.

Even projectiles designed to expand and that are fired at supersonic velocities often fail. From left to right are Super Vel 180 gr. JHP (recovered from mule deer), Remington 240 gr. JSP (recovered from elk) and Keith type 250 gr. SWC shown for comparison purposes. Nominal velocities from 6" S&W Model 29 revolver were 1490 and 1325 fps respectively. Why the heavier bullet upset and the lighter one did not is one of the dangerous mysteries of the profession.

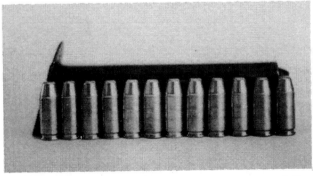

Firepower is a military term connotating squad fire and maneuver tactics with military weapons, not handguns, used in the offensive mode. To reduce the power and size of the ammunition involved to allow carrying of increased quantities smacks of a loss of perspective.

HATCHER'S TABLE OF RELATIVE STOPPING POWER

CARTRIDGE	MOMENTUM, POUNDS — FEET PER SECOND	SECTIONAL AREA OF BULLET, SQ. IN.	FACTOR FOR SHAPE AND MATERIAL	RELATIVE STOPPING POWER (RSP)
.22 Long Rifle Outdoor type	.083	.039	1000	3.3
.22 Long Rifle Hi-Speed	.097	.039	1000	3.8
.22 L.R. Hi-Speed Sharp Shoulder	.097	.039	1250	4.7
.25 ACP (6.35mm)	.083	.049	900	3.7
.30 Luger (7.65mm)	.246	.075	900	16.6
.30 Mauser (7.63mm)	.249	.075	900	16.8
.32 ACP (7.65mm)	.147	.076	900	10
.32 Smith & Wesson	.118	.076	1000	9.0
.32 Smith & Wesson Long	.165	.076	1000	12.5
.32 Colt New Police	.164	.076	1100	13.7
.32-20 (.32 Winchester)	.244	076	1100	20.3
.380 ACP (9mm short)	.177	.102	900	16.2
.38 Super	.347	102	900	31.8
.38 (9mm Luger)	.288	.102	1000	29.4
.38 Smith & Wesson	.233	.102	1000	23.8
.38 Colt New Police	.240	.102	1100	27.0
.38 Smith & Wesson Super Police	.273	.102	1050	29.2
.38 Long Colt	.272	.102	1000	27.7
.38 Smith & Wesson Special	.302	.102	1000	30.8
.38 Colt Special	.302	.102	1100	33.3
.38 Special Super Police	.338	.102	1050	36.3
.38/44 Smith & Wesson Special	.386	.102	1000	39.4
.38 Colt Special High Velocity	.386	.102	1100	43.3
.38/44 Special Keith bullet	.386	.102	1250	49.2
.38-40 (.38 Winchester)	.380	.126	1100	52.6
.41 Long Colt	.305	.129	1050	41.8
.44 Smith & Wesson Special	.416	.146	1000	60.6
.44-40 (.44 Winchester)	.408	.143	1100	64.2
.45 ACP	.420	.159	900	60.0
.45 Colt, 770 fps velocity	.428	.163	1050	73.6
.45 Colt, 910 fps velocity	.505	.163	1100	87.4

HATCHER SCALE

Cal. .36 Bullet Factor = 1. Lead Round Nose Bullet .380 ACP, 9mm Parabellum, .38 Special, .38 Super and .357 Magnum cartridges.

WGT. VEL.	95	100	105	110	115	120	125	130	135	140	145	150	155	160	165
800	17	18	19	20	21	22	23	24	24	25	26	27	28	29	30
825	18	19	20	21	21	22	23	24	25	26	27	28	29	30	31
850	18	19	20	21	22	23	24	25	26	27	28	29	30	31	32
875	19	20	21	22	23	24	25	26	27	28	29	30	31	32	33
900	19	20	21	22	23	24	25	27	28	29	30	31	32	33	34
925	20	21	22	23	24	25	26	27	28	29	30	31	32	33	34
950	20	22	23	24	25	26	27	28	29	30	31	32	33	34	35
975	21	22	23	24	25	27	28	29	30	31	32	33	34	35	36
1000	22	23	24	25	26	27	28	29	31	32	33	34	35	36	37
1025	22	23	24	26	27	28	29	30	31	33	34	35	36	37	38

WT. VEL.	95	100	105	110	115	120	125	130	135	140	145	150	155	160	165
1050	23	24	25	26	27	29	30	31	32	33	34	36	37	38	39
1075	23	24	26	27	28	29	30	32	33	34	35	37	38	39	40
1100	24	25	26	27	29	30	31	32	34	35	36	37	39	40	41
1125	24	25	27	28	29	31	32	33	34	36	37	38	40	41	42
1150	25	26	27	29	30	31	33	34	35	36	38	39	40	42	43
1175	25	27	28	29	31	32	33	35	36	37	39	40	41	43	44
1200	26	27	29	30	31	33	34	35	37	38	39	41	42	43	45
1225	26	28	29	31	32	33	35	36	37	39	40	42	43	44	46
1250	27	28	30	31	33	34	35	37	38	40	41	42	44	45	47
1275	27	29	30	32	33	35	36	38	39	40	42	43	45	46	48

WGT. VEL.	95	100	105	110	115	120	125	130	135	140	145	150	155	160	165
1300	28	29	31	32	34	36	37	38	40	41	43	44	46	47	49
1325	29	30	32	33	35	36	38	39	41	42	44	45	47	48	50
1350	29	31	32	34	35	37	38	40	41	43	44	46	47	49	50
1375	30	31	33	34	36	37	39	40	42	44	45	47	48	50	51
1400	30	32	33	35	36	38	40	41	43	44	46	48	49	51	52
1425	31	32	34	36	37	39	40	42	44	45	47	48	50	52	53
1450	31	33	34	36	38	39	41	43	44	46	48	49	51	53	54
1475	32	33	35	37	38	40	42	43	45	47	48	50	52	53	55
1500	32	34	36	37	39	41	42	44	46	48	49	51	53	54	56
1525	33	35	36	38	40	41	43	45	47	48	50	52	54	55	57

HATCHER'S SCALE

Cal. .45 Bullet Factor = 1. Lead Round Nose Bullet .45 ACP, .45 Colt cartridges.

WGT VEL.	185	190	195	200	205	210	215	220	225	230	235	240	245	250	255
700	46	47	48	49	51	52	53	54	56	57	58	59	61	62	63
710	46	48	49	50	51	53	54	55	56	58	59	60	61	63	64
720	47	48	50	51	52	53	55	56	57	58	60	61	62	64	65
730	48	49	50	52	53	54	55	57	58	59	61	62	63	64	66
740	48	50	51	52	54	55	56	57	59	60	61	63	64	65	67
750	49	50	52	53	54	56	57	58	60	61	62	64	65	66	68
760	50	51	52	54	55	56	58	59	60	62	63	64	66	67	68
770	50	52	53	54	56	57	58	60	61	63	64	65	67	68	69
780	51	52	54	55	56	58	59	61	62	63	65	66	67	69	70
790	52	53	54	56	57	59	60	61	63	64	66	67	68	70	71
WGT VEL.	**185**	**190**	**195**	**200**	**205**	**210**	**215**	**220**	**225**	**230**	**235**	**240**	**245**	**250**	**255**
800	52	54	55	57	58	59	61	62	64	65	66	68	69	71	72
810	53	54	56	57	59	60	62	63	64	66	67	69	70	72	73
820	54	55	56	58	59	61	62	64	65	67	68	69	71	72	73
830	54	56	57	59	60	62	63	64	66	67	69	70	72	73	75
840	55	56	58	59	61	62	64	65	67	68	70	71	73	74	76
850	56	57	59	60	62	63	65	66	68	69	71	72	74	75	77
860	56	58	59	61	62	64	65	67	68	70	71	73	74	76	77
870	57	58	60	61	63	65	66	68	69	71	72	74	75	77	78
880	57	59	61	62	64	65	67	68	70	71	73	75	76	78	79
890	58	60	61	63	64	66	68	69	71	72	74	75	77	79	80
WGT VEL.	**185**	**190**	**195**	**200**	**205**	**210**	**215**	**220**	**225**	**230**	**235**	**240**	**245**	**250**	**255**
900	59	60	62	64	65	67	68	70	72	73	75	76	78	79	81
910	59	61	63	64	66	67	69	71	72	74	76	77	79	80	82
920	60	62	63	65	67	68	70	71	73	75	76	78	80	81	83
930	61	62	64	66	67	69	71	72	74	76	77	79	80	82	84
940	61	63	65	66	68	70	71	73	75	76	78	80	81	83	85
950	62	64	65	67	69	70	72	74	75	77	79	81	82	84	86
960	63	64	66	68	69	71	73	75	76	78	80	81	83	85	86
970	63	65	67	69	70	72	74	75	77	79	80	82	84	86	87
980	64	66	67	69	71	73	74	76	78	80	81	83	85	87	88
990	65	66	68	70	72	73	75	77	79	80	82	84	86	87	89
WGT VEL.	**185**	**190**	**195**	**200**	**205**	**210**	**215**	**220**	**225**	**230**	**235**	**240**	**245**	**250**	**255**
1000	65	67	69	71	72	74	76	78	79	81	83	85	87	88	90
1010	66	68	70	71	73	75	77	78	80	82	84	86	87	89	91
1020	67	68	70	72	74	76	77	79	81	83	85	86	88	90	92
1030	67	69	71	73	75	76	78	80	82	84	85	87	89	91	93
1040	68	70	72	73	75	77	79	81	83	84	86	88	90	92	94
1050	69	70	72	74	76	78	80	82	83	85	87	89	91	93	95
1060	69	71	73	75	77	79	80	82	84	86	88	90	92	94	95
1070	70	72	74	76	77	79	81	83	85	87	89	91	93	94	96
1080	71	72	74	76	78	80	82	84	86	88	90	92	93	95	97
1090	71	73	75	77	79	81	83	85	87	89	90	92	94	96	98
WGT VEL.	**185**	**190**	**195**	**200**	**205**	**210**	**215**	**220**	**225**	**230**	**235**	**240**	**245**	**250**	**255**
1100	72	74	76	78	80	82	84	85	87	89	91	93	95	97	99
1110	73	74	76	78	80	82	84	86	88	90	92	94	96	98	100
1120	73	75	77	79	81	83	85	87	89	91	93	95	97	99	101
1130	74	76	78	80	82	84	86	88	90	92	94	96	98	100	102
1140	74	76	79	81	83	85	87	89	91	93	95	97	99	101	103
1150	75	77	79	81	83	85	87	89	91	93	95	97	99	102	104
1160	76	78	80	82	84	86	88	90	92	94	96	98	100	102	104
1170	76	79	81	83	85	87	89	91	93	95	97	99	101	103	105
1180	77	79	81	83	85	88	90	92	94	96	98	100	102	104	106
1190	78	80	82	84	86	88	90	92	95	97	99	101	103	105	107

at 1100 fps and a lead one at 705 fps. People just aren't built of gelatin blocks and regardless of the material involved, aren't composed of a solid mass of anything, rather they are composed of layers of alternating bone, skin, muscle, membrane, etc. I have a file full of frangible bullets taken from living organisms, including people, that didn't upset at all, even at impact velocities exceeding Mach 1. Why? Easy — everything depends upon *what the*

bullet hits during its passage. It's just that simple. If nothing of major resistance is struck — no upset, at least at handgun velocities. A 150 grain .30-06 bullet travelling at 2800 fps — you bet, but not at handgun velocities.

In general, JSP and JHP bullets will, if sufficiently frangible and if travelling at speeds past Mach 1, and if they strike something solid, upset about half (50%) of the time. Placing this entire

TAYLOR SIMPLIFIED SHORT FORM

No.	Cartridge	Bullet/Wt.	Barrel Length	Velocity	Bore Factor	Expand?	RSP
1.	.22 Long Rifle	LRN — 45 gr.	3.0	940	.039	NO	1.70
2.	.25 ACP (6.35)	FMC — 50 gr.	3.0	820	.049	NO	2.05
3.	.32 ACP (7.65)	FMC — 71 gr.	3.75	870	.075	NO	4.63
4.	.38 S&W (.357)	LRN — 146 gr.	4.0	680	.102	NO	9.93
5.	.380 ACP	FMC — 95 gr.	3.5	899	.102	NO	8.54
	(9mm K)	JHP — 90 gr.	3.5	970	.102	NO	8.73
6.	.38 Super	FMC — 130 gr.	5.0	1185	.102	YES	15.40
	(.355)	JHP — 115 gr.	5.0	1242	.102	YES	19.38*/14.27
7.	.38 Spl. (.357)	JHP — 95 gr.	4.0	1050	.102	NO	9.98
		JHP — 110 gr.	4.0	1085	.102	NO	11.94
		JHP — 125 gr.	4.0	1040	.102	NO	13.00
		JHP — 140 gr.	4.0	1040	.102	NO	14.56
		LRN — 158 gr.	4.0	824	.102	NO	13.02
		LHBWC — 148 gr.	4.0	622	.102	NO	9.21
8.	9mm Para (.355)	JHP — 90 gr.	4.25	1390	.102	YES	15.64*/12.51
		JHP — 100 gr.	4.25	1270	.102	YES	15.87*/12.70
		JHP — 115 gr.	4.25	1200	.102	YES	17.25*/13.80
		FMC — 124 gr.	4.25	1090	.102	NO	13.64
		JSP — 125 gr.	4.25	1110	.102	YES	17.33*/13.87
9.	.357 Magnum	JHP — 110 gr.	4.0	1370	.102	YES	18.84*/15.07
	(.357)	JHP — 125 gr.	4.0	1380	.102	YES	21.57*/17.25
		JHP — 140 gr.	4.0	1120	.102	YES	19.30*/15.68
		JHP — 158 gr.	4.0	1020	.102	NO	16.12
10.	.41 Police	LSWC — 210 gr.	4.0	970	.132	NO	27.09
	(.410)						
11.	.41 Magnum	JHP — 210 gr.	4.0	1240	.132	YES	43.28*/34.63
	(.410)						
12.	.44 Spl. (.429)	LRN — 246 gr.	4.0	690	.143	NO	25.46
13.	.44 Magnum	JHP — 180 gr.	4.0	1440	.143	YES	48.50*/38.80
	(.429)	JHP — 200 gr.	4.0	1310	.143	YES	49.12*/39.30
		JHP — 240 gr.	4.0	1109	.143	YES	49.50*/39.60
14.	.45 ACP	JSWC — 185 gr.	5.0	775	.163	NO	23.80
	(11.45)(.452)	JHP — 190 gr.	5.0	1001	.163	NO	31.57
		JHP — 200 gr.	5.0	960	.163	NO	31.87
		JRN — 230 gr.	5.0	828	.163	NO	31.61
15.	.45 Colt (.454)	LFP — 255 gr.	4.0	804	.163	NO	34.03

Abbreviations:

LRN = Lead Round Nose

JSWC = Jacketed Semi-Wadcutter

LFP = Lead Flat Point

JHP = Jacketed Hollow Point

FMC = Full Metal Case

JSP = Jacketed Soft Point

LHBWC = Lead Hollow Base Wadcutter

* Denotes RSP if bullet does indeed expand. Second figure indicates RSP if bullet does **not** expand.

A MINIMUM "SCORE" OF 20.00 IS "PASS-ING", i.e., 85% + probability of a 1 shot "stop" with a solid torso hit.

BORE AREA IN INCHES (ROUNDED TO NEAREST DECIMAL)

CALIBER		BORE AREA
.355	.099	.0989
.357	.1	.1000
.36	.102	.1017
.4	.126	.1256
.41	.132	.1320
.44	.152	.1520
.45	.159	.1590
.452	.16	.1604

MOMENTUM WEIGHT/VELOCITY EQUIVALENTS

Momentum weight and velocity equivalents based on a 115 gr. bullet at 1150 feet per second

WEIGHT	VELOCITY
90	1469
95	1392
100	1323
105	1260
110	1202
115	1150
120	1102
125	1058
130	1017
135	980
140	945
145	912
150	882
155	853
160	827
165	802
170	778
175	756
180	735
185	715
190	696
195	678
200	661
205	645
210	630
215	615
220	601
225	588
230	575
235	563
240	551
245	540
250	529

Momentum weight and velocity equivalents based on a 230 grain bullet at 825 feet per second

WEIGHT	VELOCITY
90	2108
95	1997
100	1898
105	1807
110	1725
115	1650
120	1581
125	1518
130	1460
135	1406
140	1355
145	1309
150	1265
155	1224
160	1186
165	1150
170	1116
175	1084
180	1054
185	1026
190	999
195	973
200	949
205	926
210	904
215	883
220	863
225	843
230	825
235	807
240	791
245	774
250	759

matter into its proper perspective . . . how can one determine into which half of the probability factor his particular fight will fall? Hmm, that's a problem worth seriously considering, is it not?

A quick glance at my "Modified Short Form" above will also disclose the true velocities of which the .38 Special, 9mm Parabellum and .357 Magnum are capable with service length barrels. A few moments of cogitation on those velocities will disclose that reliable bullet expansion is all but impossible with *any* form of .38 Special, not a certainty with 9mm Parabellum and only possible with the .357 Magnum when barrel lengths of at least 4 inches are used and only then with certain loads.

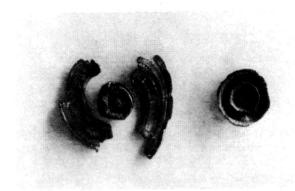

Home brewed 148 gr. hollow based wadcutter loaded backwards with a heavy charge of Unique powder. At left is .357 at about 1170 fps and at right is .38 Special at about 700 fps. Bullets were recovered from whitetailed deer.

148 gr. HBWC loaded backwards recovered from a human.

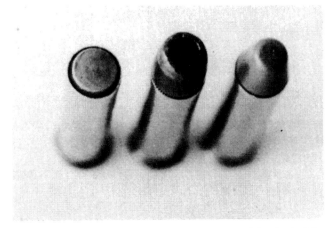

Special purpose ammunition often fulfills desirable functions. From left to right are Glaser Safety Slug .357, Hydra-Shok .357 and KTW metal piercing .357.

The 1935 specs for the .357 were obtained in 8-3/8" barrels, with loads that far exceed those currently deemed safe. This is why "modern" .357's aren't what they are proclaimed to be in the performance department. They are, however, over-penetrative, produce excessive muzzle blast and flash, and recoil far too much to be readily controllable in fast combat DA work. Careful selection of barrel length and the type of load utilized in that barrel is the ticket to success with the .357 "Magnum".

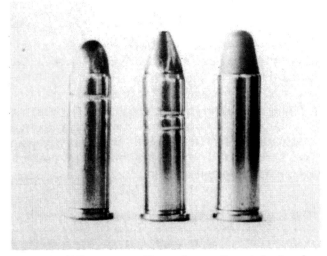

Several different configurations of metal piercing bullets are available for special purpose use. Left to right: Remington 158 gr. JRN, Winchester 158 gr. MP and KTW metal piercing. All cartridges are .38 Special.

To illuminate further the issue, generally expect to lose an average of about 100 feet per second velocity per inch of barrel lost, starting with 8-3/8" as a beginning point. Using this information, extrapolation of true velocities with various bullet weights in particular barrel lengths and how those velocities affect bullet expansion, are not difficult. In simple terms — be careful with the .357.

In contrast, the 255 gr. lead flatnose bullet of the .45 Colt, for example (255/804 fps) is quite satisfactory for manstopping duty (34.03 on the Taylor Modified Short Form — 87.4 on Hatcher's Scale). Yet it is easy to control, quite accurate, not overly penetrative and is used in a gun that doesn't say "Magnum" on it anywhere . . . a distinct asset in the public relations oriented world of law enforcement.

Watch for the term "killing power", for it is constantly bantered about during discussions of stopping power. We are not primarily interested

Although factory ammunition is far more reliable in its performance and quality control than any handload can be, mishaps sometimes occur. For this reason, any ammo that is carried should be visually inspected. Left to right: bullet has no lead core . . . only a jacket, center cartridge has improperly seated bullet with resultantly bulged case, cartridge at right sports mashed case mouth obtained during bullet seating.

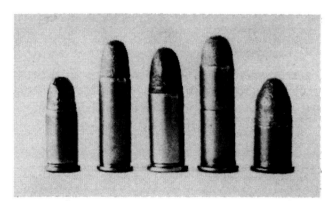

Cartridges of the black powder era that can still be found, sometimes in smokeless powder loadings are (left to right): .32 Short Colt, .32 Long Colt, .38 S&W, .38 Long Colt and .41 Rimfire. All are extremely poor manstoppers and should be avoided if the protagonist has any choice at all.

in *killing* anyone by shooting him with our defensive handgun . . . only *stopping* him. Certainly a wound which stops him may also kill him — *but not necessarily.* More than 50% of those who are shot and stopped are *not* killed. Lethality of a given cartridge is not the issue or we could all use .22's and not worry about it.

Remember that one can render a mortal wound on his adversary and *not stop him.* He may die minutes, hours, days or even weeks later in the hospital, but that does you no good at all if he kills you first! This is why the difference between lethality and incapacitation must be defined and understood.

I am in no way saying that only big bore handguns are worth considering for defensive employment. I am saying that the smaller calibers fail to stop more often, *much* more often in fact, than the larger ones. This means only that the parameters within which the weapon must be used to have positive effect are narrower with the small calibers. I would rather have a woman carry a .32 auto in her purse than leave her .45 at home! Case/Point?

In conclusion, the objective consideration of all the current "in vogue" theories demands that Hatcher's postulations on momentum be given prime emphasis, regardless of the fact that they were formulated over 40 years ago. No amount of "slide rule engineering" has provided us with a more valid explanation. I have literally bet my life on weapons and ammunition selected as a direct result of confidence in Hatcher's opinions with (so far!) extraordinarily successful results.

When the stakes are high, you owe it to yourself to be very, *very* careful.

Sampling of cartridges used mostly in auto pistols that produce unsatisfactory stopping power results. Left to right: .25 ACP ball, .25 ACP KTW metal piercing (!), .32 ACP (7.65mm), .32 MAB (7.65mm), .30 Luger (Parabellum), 7.62x25mm Tokarev (7.63 Mauser) and .38 ACP.

ADDENDA TO CHAPTER 6

CALIBER/PROJECTILE PENETRATION TESTS

CARTRIDGE	MFR., BULLET & WEIGHT	GUN, BARREL LENGTH	BOARDS PENETRATED
.22 Long	Remington — copper plated	.22 Conversion Unit	3-1/2
.22 Long Rifle	Remington — copper plated	"	5-1/2
.25 Auto	WW 50 gr. FMC	Sterling, 2-3/8"	4-1/3
.38 Special	SPEER HOT Shot	S&W Chief Model 66, 2" barrel	1/2*
	Rem. 125 gr. SJHP	"	4-1/2
	Rem. 158 gr. lead	"	3-3/4
	Speer 158 gr. JHP	"	4-1/4
	SCORPION Hydra-Shok	"	2-1/3
	WW 150 gr. Metal Piercing	"	6-1/3
	KTW Metal Piercing	"	8
9mm Parabellum	WW 115 gr. FMC	Star, 3.9"	9-1/2
	KTW Metal Penetrating	"	11-2/3
.38 Super	WW 125 gr. JHP	Colt Govt. Model, 5"	7
	KTW Metal Penetrating	"	12
.44 Special	Remington 246 gr. lead	Charter Arms Bulldog, 3"	4-7/8
	"	Ruger .44 Mag, 7-1/2"	7
	KTW Metal Penetrating	"	8-1/3
.44 Magnum	Remington 240 gr. SP	Ruger .44 Mag., 7-1/2"	12
	Speer Hot Shot	"	2-1/8
.45 Auto	Federal 185 gr. JHP	Colt. Govt. Model, 5"	6-1/2
	WW 185 gr. STHP	HARDBALLER Long Slide, 7"	6-1/3
	Remington 185 gr. HP	"	7-1/2
	WW 185 gr. HP	Colt Govt. Model, 5"	6-1/2
	Speer 200 gr. JHP	"	6-1/4
	Hornady 230 gr. FFMJ	"	7-1/4
	WW 230 gr. FMC	"	8-7/8
	"	Colt Commander, 4¼"	8-1/2
	KTW 182 gr. Metal Penetrating	Colt Govt. Model, 5"	9-1/2
	"	HARDBALLER Long Slide, 7"	10-1/2
	WW Highway Master MP	Colt Govt. Model, 5"	11-1/2

* 1/2 of the board was penetrated and energy split the board the rest of the way through. No pellets reached the second board.

TRANSCRIPT OF ACTION REPORT
FAILURE TO STOP — .357 MAGNUM

Legend:
  a. Offense — Deadly Assault On a Peace Officer.
  b. Time — 1:48 A.M.
  c. Weapon Used — Butcher knife.
  d. Number of Officers Involved — 2, one regular, one reserve.
  e. How Reported — Police Mobile Radio.
  f. Suspect Data — White, Male, age 23.
  g. Police Weapon — S&W Model 19, .357 Magnum, 4 inch barrel.
  h. Ammunition — Remington .357 Magnum, 125 gr. JHP.
  i. Participants — Police Officer No. 1, Police Officer No. 2, Police Dispatcher, Police Sergeant, Suspect and Suspect's Wife.

Sequence of Action:

1:44 A.M., *Dispatcher* receives telephone call from *unidentified female* who states, "Hello, can you send a police car to my residence (gives address)?"

Dispatcher asks: "What is the problem?"

Female replies: "I think my husband has had a nervous breakdown."

Dispatcher asks: "What is he doing?"

Female responds, "I don't know!" — then screams, "Honey, don't!" She then drops the telephone receiver and was heard running away screaming. At this time telephone contact was lost.

Dispatcher sends patrol unit, occupied by *Officer No. 1* and Reserve *Officer No. 2*, working beat No. 303, on a Signal 15, domestic disturbance call, to address given *by female*. *Police Sergeant*, patrol unit No. 302, was dispatched to assist at 1:45 A.M.

While the two patrol units were enroute to the scene, *dispatcher* cross-checked address given by female in city directory and obtained the name listed with the telephone number for the address given by *female*. He then telephoned that number and the *suspect* answered. *Dispatcher* asks if *female* (suspect's wife) is there. *Suspect* answers, "She's not here. Can I help you?" *Dispatcher* asks *suspect* if he is suspect by name, at which time *suspect* advises, "Yes." *Dispatcher* attempts to confirm the address, to which *suspect* responds, "You must have the wrong number, " and hangs up.

Dispatcher notifies responding patrol units of telephone conversation with *suspect* via radio. (*Suspect's wife* later told officets that suspect was present in the kitchen when she told him, "I'm going to call the police." To which *suspect* responded, "Go ahead and call.")

1:48 A.M., *Officers No. 1 and 2* arrive at the address provided earlier by *dispatcher*. They observe a white male dressed only in white underwear shorts standing near a small tree in the dark, located in the front yard of the residence. *Suspect* was observed to be holding an unidentified object in his hand.

Officer No. 1 dismounts from patrol vehicle and approaches curb at suspect's residence. He orders

suspect to step out. *Suspect* starts to move towards officer. He is observed at this time to be holding a large refrigerator drawer full of potatoes and a large *butcher knife*. *Officer No. 1* orders *suspect* to stop, at which time *suspect* throws drawer full of said potatoes at *Officer No. 1* and, armed with *butcher knife*, lunges at him, stabbing him in the abdomen. *Officer No. 1* draws his service revolver, a .357 Magnum S&W revolver, loaded with Remington 125 gr. JHP ammunition, and orders *suspect*, "Stop, man!" *Suspect* continues to stab *Officer No. 1* with the knife. *Officer No. 1* was backpeddling as this action continued. At the point which both *Officer No. 1* and *suspect* reached the street, *Officer No. 1* fired his service weapon in self-defense, striking *suspect* twice in the center of the chest.

At this time, *Officer No. 2*, a reserve officer (unarmed), notifies *dispatcher* via radio, "Officer needs assistance, shots fired!" *Suspect*, after being shot twice in the chest, continues attacking *Officer No. 1*, with no visible let-up. *Officer No. 1* received a total of 9 wounds, and collapsed in the driveway of *suspect's residence* approximately 5 feet from the street curb. *Suspect* was standing over *Officer No. 1* when *Officer No. 2* (unarmed reserve officer) went towards *suspect* attempting to strike him (unsuccessfully) with his fists. *Suspect* then stood up and turned towards *Officer No. 2*, who is now under the impression that *suspect* has possession of *Officer No. 1*'s service revolver, and begins backing away. *Officer No. 2* lures *suspect* into chasing him down the street to get him away from *Officer No. 1* who is by now seriously wounded. The chase covers a distance of about 100 yards during which *Officer No. 2* eludes *suspect*.

1:49 A.M., *Sergeant* arrives on the scene and observes *Officer No. 1* seriously wounded at the suspect's address, bleeding copiously from his wounds, crouched in the front yard. *Sergeant* places the officer in the back seat of his patrol unit and instructs the still-conscious officer to apply pressure to the wounds as best he can.

Sergeant then notices *suspect* lying in the street approximately 4 ft. from the street curb adjacent to the empty lot next door to *suspect's residence*, in a large pool of blood. Two gunshot wounds are observed in *suspect's* chest.

Sergeant notifies *dispatcher* via radio to send an ambulance to *suspect's* residence. He also advises *dispatcher* that he will be enroute to hospital with injured *Officer No. 1* at 1:52 A.M.

Officer No. 3, in unit No. 305, arrives at suspect's residence at 1:53 A.M., discovering that *suspect* was now gone from pool of blood in street and begins a search for him. It was unknown at this time if *suspect* was still armed. *Officer No. 3* observes *suspect standing* in the front yard of adjacent residence and orders him to lie down. *Suspect* refuses to do so. *Officer No. 3* forcibly takes him down after finding him to be unarmed.

Suspect continues to struggle, striking *Officer No. 3* with his hands and feet. *Officer No. 3* handcuffs *suspect* to assist in controlling him. A fire department ambulance attendant, who had heard shots and come to the scene in his private vehicle arrives and assists *Officer No. 3* in controlling *suspect* until

ambulance arrives at 2:06 A.M.

Suspect is then transported to hospital.

Subsequent investigation determined that *suspect* was still struggling upon arrival at the hospital, whereupon he was placed in critical condition listing and admitted. He died *two weeks* later of his wounds.

Suspect's butcher knife was recovered from pool of blood in street.

Officer No. 1 recovered from his wounds and eventually returned to duty.

Investigation was continued and brought to a close in the normal manner by *Officer No. 2* who had returned to the crime scene, with assistance from *Sergeant*, who had returned to the crime scene.

SPECIFICATIONS FOR POPULAR HANDGUN DEFENSIVE CARTRIDGES

.380 ACP (aka 9mm Kurz, 9mm Corto)

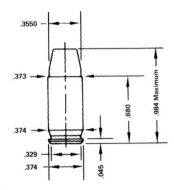

Bullet Diameter: .355
Available Bullet Weights: 80 gr., 88 gr., 95 gr.
Bullet Configurations Available: Ball, LRN, JHP.
Nominal Velocity with Standard (95 gr.) Bullet: 900 fps.

Typical Handguns in Which Used:
  Walther PPK
  Walther PPK/s
  Walther PP
  Mauser HSC
  Beretta M1934
  Astra Constable
  AMT Backup
  Beretta M70S
  Bernardelli M80
  Star Super SM
  Sterling M400

9mm Parabellum (9x19, 9mm Luger)

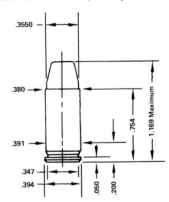

Bullet Diameter: .355
Available Bullet Weights: 80 gr., 88 gr., 90 gr., 100 gr., 108 gr., 115 gr., 124 gr.
Bullet Configurations Available: Ball, AP, TR, LRN, JSP, JHP, SWC, Blank.
Nominal Velocity with Standard (124 gr. Ball) Bullet: 900 - 1020 fps.

Typical Handguns in Which Used:

  Luger P-08
  Walther P-38
  Browning P-35 (Hi-Power)
  Radom
  Broomhandle Mauser
  Heckler & Koch P-7

Heckler & Koch VP-70
Smith & Wesson M39
Smith & Wesson M59
Brno CZ-75
Beretta 92s-1

.38 Super Automatic

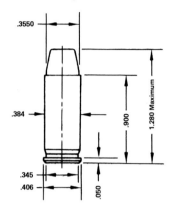

Bullet diameter: .355/9mm
Available Bullet Weights: All 9mm types, plus 130 gr. Ball.
Bullet Configurations Available: Same as 9mm Parabellum.
Nominal Velocity with Standard (130 gr. Ball) Bullet: 1170 fps.

Typical Handguns in Which Used:

> Colt Government Model
> Star
> Llama
> Astra

.38 Special

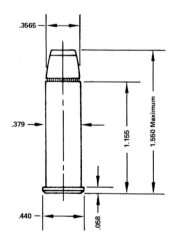

Bullet Diameter: .357
Available Bullet Weights: 90 gr., 100 gr., 110 gr.,

125 gr., 140 gr., 146 gr., 148 gr., 150 gr., 158 gr., 160 gr., 200 gr.
Bullet Configurations Available: Ball, LRN, SWC, JSP, JHP, JFP, WC.
Nominal Velocity with Standard (158 gr. LRN) Bullet: 840 fps.

Typical Handguns in Which Used:

> Colt Detective Special
> Colt Cobra
> Colt Diamondback
> Smith & Wesson M10, M12, M14, M15, M36, M49, M60, M67.
> Dan Wesson
> Charter Arms Undercover
> Ruger Security Six
> Ruger Speed Six

.357 Magnum

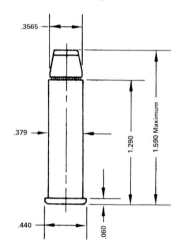

Bullet Diameter: .357
Available Bullet Weights: All .38 Special weights (bullet is identical).
Bullet Configurations Available: All the same as with .38 Special.
Nominal Velocity with Standard (158 gr.) Bullet: 8-3/8" bbl = 1370 fps, 6" bbl = 1260 fps, 5" bbl = 1130 fps, 4" bbl = 1020 fps, 3-1/2" bbl = 970 fps, 2-1/2" bbl = 920 fps.

Typical Handguns in Which Used:

> Colt Python
> Colt Trooper
> Colt Lawman

Smith & Wesson M19, M13, M27, M28, M65, M66
Ruger Security Six
Dan Wesson

.41 Magnum

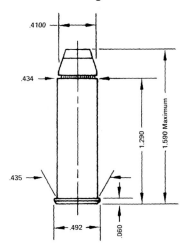

Bullet Diameter: .410
Available Bullet Weights: 210 gr., 225 gr.
Bullet Configurations Available: SWC, JSP, JHP.
Nominal Velocity with Standard (225 gr. JSP) Bullet: 1370 fps.

Typical Handguns in Which Used:

Smith & Wesson M57, M58

.44 Special

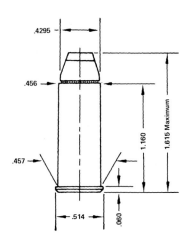

Bullet Diameter: .429
Available Bullet Weights: 180 gr., 200 gr., 215 gr., 225 gr., 240 gr., 246 gr., 250 gr., 265 gr.

Bullet Configurations Available: LRN, SWC, JHP, JSP, JFP.
Nominal Velocity with Standard (246 gr. LRN) Bullet: 750 fps.

Typical Handguns in Which Used:

Smith & Wesson M20, M21, M24

.44 Magnum

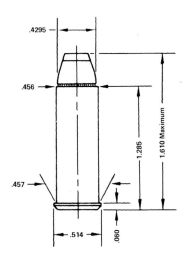

Bullet Diameter: .429
Available Bullet Weights: Same as .44 Special.
Bullet Configurations Available: Same as .44 Spl.
Nominal Velocity with Standard (240 gr. JSP) Bullet: 1410 fps (8-3/8" bbl).

Typical Handguns in Which Used:

Smith & Wesson M 29
High Standard Crusader
Ruger Redhawk

.45 Auto Rim

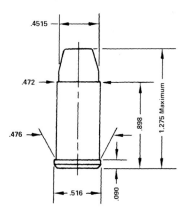

Bullet Diameter: .451

Available Bullet Weights: Same as .45 ACP.
Bullet Configurations Available: Same as .45 ACP.
Nominal Velocity with Standard (230 gr. Ball) Bullet: 825 fps.

Typical Handguns in Which Used:

Colt M1917
Smith & Wesson M1917

.45 ACP (aka .45 Auto)

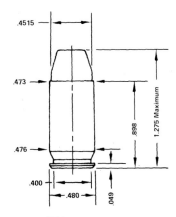

Bullet Diameter: .451
Available Bullet Weights: 190 gr., 200 gr., 215 gr., 230 gr.
Bullet Configurations Available: LRN, Ball, JSP, JHP, JFP, SWC.
Nominal Velocity with Standard (230 gr. Ball) Bullet: 820 fps.

Typical Handguns in Which Used:

Colt Government Model
Colt Commander

Colt Combat Commander
Star PD
Star Model P
Semmerling
Detonics
Safari Arms Enforcer
Smith & Wesson M25
Smith & Wesson M1917
Colt M1917

.45 Colt

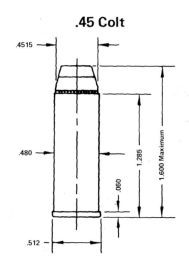

Bullet Diameter: .451, .454
Available Bullet Weights: 240 gr., 250 gr., 255 gr.
Bullet Configurations Available: SWC, JSP, JHP, LRN.
Nominal Velocity with Standard (250 gr. LRN) Bullet: 870 fps.

Typical Handguns in Which Used:

Smith & Wesson M25-5

SAMPLE CHART — BALLISTIC COEFFICIENTS

Bullet	Sectional Density	Ballistic Coefficient	Velocity (fps)
90 gr. .355 Jacketed Hollow Cavity	.102	.095	1400
		.108	900
115 gr. .355 Jacketed Hollow Cavity	.130	.127	1400
		.153	1000
		.129	700
110 gr. .357 Jacketed Hollow Cavity	.123	.116	1500
		.132	1000
125 gr. .357 Jacketed Soft Point	.140	.133	1400
		.152	1000
125 gr. .Jacketed Hollow Cavity	.140	.133	1400
		.153	1000
150 gr. Jacketed Hollow Cavity	.168	.167	1235
		.145	900
158 gr. .357 Jacketed Soft Point	.177	.175	1200
		.159	900

Bullet	Sectional Density	Ballistic Coefficient	Velocity (fps)
170 gr. .357 Full Metal Jacket Silhouette	.191	.174	1500
		.284	1000
		.222	800
170 gr. .410 Jacketed Hollow Cavity	.144	.123	1525
		.122	1180
210 gr. .410 Jacketed Hollow Cavity	.178	.165	1300
		.209	1000
180 gr. .4295 Jacketed Hollow Cavity	.139	.133	1575
		.126	1225
		.138	925
240 gr. .4295 Jacketed Hollow Cavity	.186	.185	1400
		.172	1200
		.171	800
185 gr. .4515 ACP Jacketed Hollow Cavity	.130	.110	1200
		.134	800
240 gr. .4515 Long Colt Jacketed Hollow Cavity	.168	.158	1150
		.168	800

CENTER FIRE HANDGUN CARTRIDGES OF THE WORLD

Cartridge	Case type	Bullet diameter	Neck diameter	Shoulder diameter	Base diameter	Rim diameter	Case length	Cartridge length	Twist	Primer
2.7mm Kolibri	D	.107	.139	—	.140	.140	0.37	0.43		B
3mm Kolibri	D	.120	.150	—	.150	.150	0.32	0.43		B
4.25mm Liliput	D	.167	.198	—	.198	.198	0.41	0.56		B
5mm Clement	C	.202	.223	.277	.281	.281	0.71	1.01		B
5mm Bergmann	D	.203	.230	—	.273	.274	0.59	0.96		B
5.5mm Velo Dog	B	.225	.248	—	.253	.308	1.12	1.35	8.2	S-B
.22 Remington Jet	A	.223	.247	.350	.376	.440	1.28	1.58	10	S
.221 Fire Ball	C	.224	.251	.355	.375	.375	1.40	1.82	14	S
.25 ACP	D	.251	.276	—	.277	.298	0.62	0.91	16	S
.256 Winchester Mag	A	.257	.277	.378	.378	.440	1.30	1.53	14	S
6.5mm Bergmann	C	.264	.289	.325	.367	.370	0.87	1.23		B
7mm Nambu	C	.280	.296	.337	.351	.359	0.78	1.06	12.5	B
7.62mm Nagant (Russian)	B	.295	.286	—	.335	.388	1.53	1.53	9.5	B
7.62mm Tokarev	C	.307	.330	.370	.380	.390	0.97	1.35	10	B
7.63mm Mauser	C	.308	.332	.370	.381	.390	0.99	1.36	7.9	S-B
.30 Borchardt	C	.307	.331	.370	.385	.390	0.99	1.34		S-B
7.63mm (7.65) Mannlicher	D	.308	.331	—	.332	.334	0.84	1.12	10	B
7.65mm (.30) Luger	C	.308	.322	.374	.388	.391	0.75	1.15	9.8	S-B
7.65mm MAB (French)	D	.309	.336	—	.327	.337	0.78	1.19		B
7.65mm Roth-Sauer	D	.301	.332	—	.335	.335	0.51	0.84	14.2	B
.32 ACP	H	.309	.336	—	.336	.354	0.68	1.03	16	S
.32 S&W	B	.312	.334	—	.335	.375	0.61	0.92	16-18	S
.32 S&W Long	B	.312	.334	—	.335	.375	0.93	1.27	16-18	S
.320 Revolver	B	.317	.320	—	.322	.350	0.62	0.90	22	B
.32 Colt	B	.313	.313	—	.318	.374	0.92	1.26	16	S
.35 S&W Auto	D	.309	.345	—	.346	.348	0.67	0.97	12	S
7.5mm Swiss Army	B	.317	.335	—	.345	.407	0.89	1.29		B
7.5mm Nagant (Swedish)	B	.325	.328	—	.350	.406	0.89	1.35	18	B
8mm Nambu	G	.320	.338	.388	.408	.413	0.86	1.25	11	B
8mm Lebel Revolver	B	.323	.350	—	.384	.400	1.07	1.44	9.5	B
8mm Roth-Steyr	D	.329	.353	—	.355	.356	0.74	1.14	10	B
9mm Glisenti	D	.355	.380	—	.392	.393	0.75	1.15	10	B
9mm Luger	D	.355	.380	—	.392	.393	0.76	1.16	9.8	S-B
9mm Bayard	D	.355	.375	—	.390	.392	0.91	1.32		B
9mm Steyr	D	.355	.380	—	.380	.381	0.90	1.30		B
9mm Browning Long	D	.355	.376	—	.384	.404	0.80	1.10	12-16	B
9mm Makarov	D	.363	.384	—	.389	.391	0.71	0.97		B
.357 Magnum	B	.357	.379	—	.379	.440	1.29	1.51	18.8	S
.380 Revolver	B	.375	.377	—	.380	.426	0.70	1.10	15.1	S-B
.38 Long Colt	B	.357	.377	—	.378	.433	1.03	1.32	16	S
.38 Special	B	.357	.379	—	.379	.440	1.16	1.55	16-18	S
.38 S&W	B	.359	.386	—	.386	.433	0.78	1.20	16-18	S
.38 Colt ACP & Super Auto	H	.358	.382	—	.383	.405	0.90	1.28	16	S
.380 ACP (9mm Browning Short)	D	.356	.373	—	.373	.374	0.68	0.98	12-16	S
.41 Long Colt	B	.386	.404	—	.405	.430	1.13	1.39	16	S
.41 Magnum	B	.410	.432	—	.433	.488	1.28	1.58	18	L
10.4mm Italian	B	.422	.444	—	.451	.505	0.89	1.25	10	B
.44 S&W American	B	.434	.438	—	.440	.506	0.91	1.44	20	L
.44 S&W Russian	B	.429	.457	—	.457	.515	0.97	1.43	20	L
11mm German Service	B	.426	.449	—	.453	.509	0.96	1.21	23	B
11mm French Ordnance	B	.425	.449	—	.460	.491	0.71	1.18	16.2	B

Cartridge	Case type	Bullet Diameter	Neck diameter	Shoulder diameter	Base diameter	Rim diameter	Case length	Cartridge length	Twist	Primer
.44 Special	B	.429	.457	—	.457	.514	1.16	1.62	20	L
.44 Magnum	B	.429	.457	—	.457	.514	1.29	1.61	20	L
.44 Colt	B	.443	.450	—	.456	.483	1.10	1.50	16	L
.44 Webley	B	.436	.470	—	.472	.503	0.69	1.10	20	L-B
.44 Bull Dog	B	.440	.470	—	.473	.503	0.57	0.95	21	S-B
11.75mm Montenegrin	B	.445	.472	—	.490	.555	1.40	1.73		B
.45 ACP	D	.452	.476	—	.476	.476	0.898	1.17	16	L
.45 Auto Rim	B	.452	.472	—	.476	.516	0.898	1.28	15-16	L
.45 Colt	B	.454	.476	—	.480	.512	1.29	1.60	16	L
.45 S&W Schofield	B	.454	.477	—	.476	.522	1.10	1.43	24	L
.45 Webley	B	.452	.471	—	.471	.504	0.82	1.15		L-B
.450 Revolver	B	.455	.475	—	.477	.510	0.69	1.10	16	L-B
.455 Enfield (.455 Colt)	B	.455	.473	—	.478	.530	0.87	1.35		L-B
.455 Webley Revolver Mk II	B	.454	.476	—	.480	.535	0.77	1.23	10	B
.455 Webley Auto	H	.455	.473	—	.474	.500	0.93	1.23	10	B
.476 Enfield	B	.472	.474	—	.478	.530	0.87	1.33		B
.50 Remington Army	A	.508	.532	.563	.565	.665	0.57	1.24		L

A - Rimmed, bottleneck   C - Rimless, bottleneck   G - Semi-rimmed, bottleneck
B - Rimmed, straight   D - Rimless, straight   H - Semi-rimmed, straight

Primer: S - Small rifle (.175")   L - Large rifle (.210")   B - Berdan type

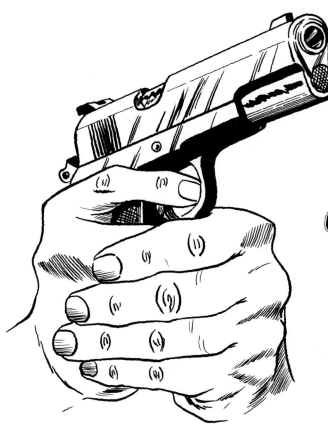

CHAPTER 7

TECHNIQUE:
How To Best Utilize
The Defensive Handgun

BASIC DRY PRACTICE DRILL

1. **Ready/Point Position, go from ready to point 20 times.**
   a. Ready Position: Locked in Weaver Stance, but with weapon pointed downward at about a 45° angle. Finger is OFF the trigger and touches the protruding button from the slide stop. Thumb safety is ON with thumb resting on top. Eyes are downrange.
   b. Point Position: Weapon is pointed at the target in solid Weaver Stance, finger is on trigger, safety is OFF, eyes focused on the front sight.

2. **Presenting The Weapon, perform 25 times.**
   a. Strong hand obtains a firing grip on the weapon, weak hand is thrust outward about 10" in front of the belt buckle. The eyes are on target.

   b. Weapon is drawn clear of holster, but is not advanced. Weak hand stays as it is in "a" above. The eyes are still on the target.
   c. Weapon is advanced to a point about halfway between the holster and the weak hand. Thumb safety is depressed by thumb of firing hand at this point, but finger stays away from trigger. Eyes are still on the target.
   d. Weapon continues forward, hands join, firing elbow and wrist are locked, eyes on the target, finger now on trigger, power in hands, arms, shoulders.
   e. Weapon is brought to eye level, the sights picked up with the eye focus shifitng from the target to the front sight. P - r - e - s - s the trigger.

3. **Right Hand Pivot, 90°. Perform 20 times.**

4. Left Hand Pivot, 90°. Perform 20 times.

5. Speed Load, perform 25 times, push for 2.0 seconds to first shot after reload.

6. Tactical Reload, perform 10 times, try for 7 seconds or less with eyes maintained on target.

7. Malfunction Clearance Drill, Positions One, Two and Three. Perform 5 times each. Position One — 2 seconds, Position 2 — 1.5 seconds and Position 3 — 6 seconds. USE DUMMY AMMUNITION.

BASIC LIVE FIRE DRILL

This program is suggested for those who have completed the Basic Defensive Handgun Course. It does not supplant handling and dry firing exercises which should be practiced 30-45 minutes dialy.

All starts are from Condition One, weapon holstered and locked, hands clasped medially, held shoulder high, or at one's sides. An assistant must be recruited for timing. It is recommended that the drill should be conducted from a concealed carry once smoothness is obtained.

1. Warmup Exercises, perform each three (3) times.
   a. 1 meter, both hands held touching shoulders of silhouette target. On command to fire, clear target, place two center hits. Time: 1.5 seconds per pair.
   b. 3 meters, 2 shots, 1.5 seconds.
   c. 10 meters, 2 shots, 2.0 seconds.
   d. 15 meters, 2 shots, 3.0 seconds.

2. Mutliples, perform three (3) times.
   a. Two silhouette targets, 5 meters, placed 2 meters apart edge to edge. 1 center hit each in 1.5 seconds.
   b. Three silhouette targets, placed 1 meter apart edge to edge. 1 center hit on each in 2.5 seconds.
   c. Four silhouette targets, placed 1 meter apart edge to edge. 1 center hit each in 3.0 seconds.

3. Pivots, Turns, Etc. Perform three (3) times.
   a. Five (5) singles, 90° right pivot, 7 meters, 1.5 seconds each.
   b. Five (5) singles, 90° left pivot, 7 meters, 1.5 seconds each.

4. Failure Drill (Mozambique). Perform three (3) times. Two in chest, come down to ready position and pause, then center hit in the head. Time: 2 seconds, pause, 2 seconds.

ADVANCED DRY PRACTICE DRILL

This program is intended to develop and maintain a high level of weapon handling skill. Drill is performed in the privacy of your own home 20-30 minutes daily. 14 rounds of inert ammo are needed.

Remember to insure that your weapon is cleared and that you have no distractions while practicing.

1. The Ready Position: 20 strokes, .6 seconds each.

2. The Draw: 20 draws from *each* of three (3) hand positions (hands clasped medially, hands held shoulder high, hands at side). 1 second par time each.

3. Pivots, Turns, Etc.
   a. Right Hand Pivot. 90°. Perform 15 times. Time: 1.2 seconds each.

   b. Left Hand Pivot, 90°. Perform 15 times. Time: 1.2 seconds each.
   c. 180° Turn. Perform 15 times. Time: 1.5 seconds each.

4. Malfunction Clearance Drills:
   a. Position One, perform 10 times. Time: 2.0 seconds each.
   b. Position Two, perform 10 times. Time: 1.5 seconds each.
   c. Position Three, perform 10 times. Time: 4.0 seconds each.

5. Stress Reloads.
   a. Speed — 10 loads, 1.5 seconds each.
   b. Tactical — 10 loads, 4.0 seconds each.

(Drills continue on page 110.)

Checking the auto pistol. The tip of the weak hand thumb is inserted inside the trigger guard, bearing against the forward portion. Index finger of the same hand is then pressed against the recoil spring plunger located beneath the muzzle and the finger and thumb are then "pinched" together, forcing

the slide to retract slightly. The cartridge in the chamber is partially withdrawn and is visible to the eye. If the chamber and/or magazine well are empty, this, too, will be visible. Care should be taken to avoid placing a finger over the muzzle for obvious reasons!

Checking the revolver. Rims of cartridges show clearly at rear of cylinder as do projectiles when chambers are viewed from a frontal side view.

Looking down the barrel is not recommended. The weapon can also easily be opened for visual inspection if required.

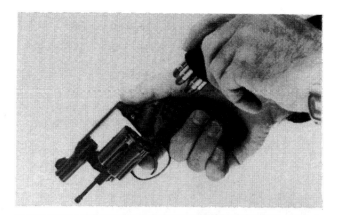

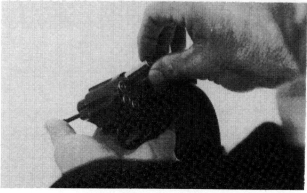

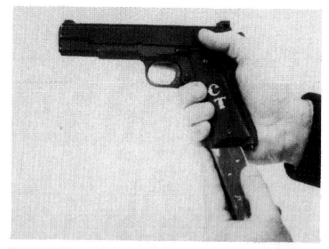

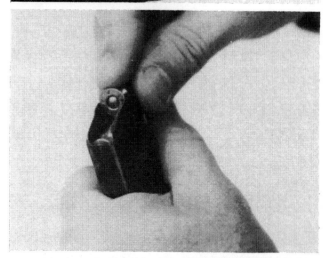

Loading the revolver: (top) with cylindrical speed loader, (center two photos) with Bianchi speed strip and (bottom) with the fingers, 2 cartridges at a time.

Loading the auto pistol: a full magazine is inserted and locked into place, then the slide is cycled once to feed the top cartridge from the magazine into the chamber. Thumb safety is then engaged, magazine withdrawn and the weapon holstered. One additional cartridge is inserted into the magazine, which is then replaced in the holstered gun and locked into place.

UNLOADING THE AUTOLOADER

Remove magazine from the gun.

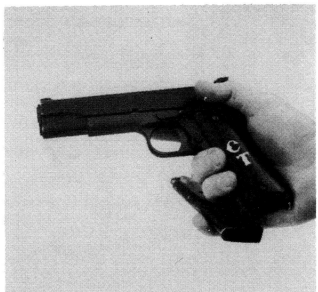

The magazine is then placed between the third and fourth finger of the firing hand to insure recognizance that it has been removed regardless of light conditions or the shooter's mental/emotional state.

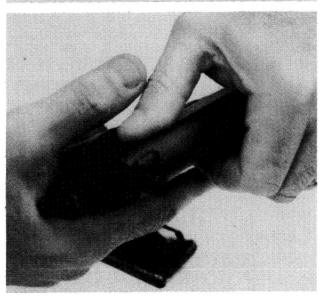

Weak hand is loosely cupped over the ejection port of the weapon. The gun is then turned on its side and the slide SLOWLY withdrawn, spilling the cartridge in the chamber into the hand. The weapon is then double checked to assure that it is indeed empty.

2.

3.

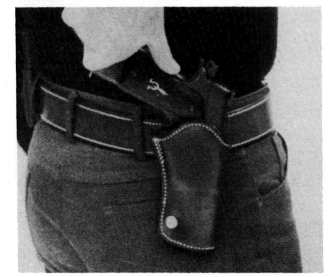

4.

1.

CHANGING MAGAZINES WHILE WEAPON IS HOLSTERED WITH CARTRIDGE IN CHAMBER
(Counterclockwise, from upper right)

1. Actuate magazine release with thumb of firing hand.

2. Exchange fresh magazine with expended or partially expended magazine.

3. Bring fresh magazine to the butt of the gun.

4. Insert magazine into magazine well.

5. Press magazine home and lock into place.

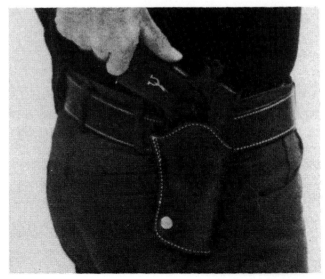

5.

THE SPEED ROCK: Torso of the body is bent backwards at the waist, weapon held just above the holster with inside of firing wrist held securely against the body. The weak hand is kept clear. This position is highly useful when an attack is sustained under such circumstances that the firer is prohibited from stepping back out of arm's reach. It should not be used under any other conditions.

FBI CROUCH: A popular law enforcement technique for many years, it can be developed into a useful technique only with a great deal of practice. It is, however, not flexible enough for employment in the great bulk of handgun altercations as far as maximum efficiency is concerned.

TWO HAND CROUCH: Developed in the early 1960's to improve control over standard one hand methods used previously. It does indeed accomplish better control, but, as with other below eye level techniques, it lacks flexibility for use under the generality of conditions usually encountered during handgun fights.

Optional supporting finger forward Weaver Grip. The author feels this to be weaker than placing all fingers of the supporting hand underneath the trigger guard.

WEAVER STANCE: Firing arm is either straight or slightly bent. The weak side shoulder is pointed toward the target, weak arm and elbow kept down at about a 50° angle. Isometric pressure is applied by the weak hand against the fingers of the strong hand to reduce muzzle jump. Designed by Los Angeles County Deputy Sheriff Jack Weaver, and developed to its full potential by Jeff Cooper, the Weaver position is the best known at the present time and far outshines any other methods.

ISOSCELES: Using sights has become popular, especially with modern police training officers. Use of sights is an important advantage in flexibility as well as accuracy.

Proper hand position with the auto pistol. Gun is straight in hand, with firing thumb held no lower than upper stock screw on left side. Even more preferable is placing the thumb on top of the thumb safety, however, depending upon the shape

of the firer's hand, depression of the grip safety may not be possible under this circumstance. If encountered, pinning the grip safety is recommended. Supporting thumb is held high, away from magazine release button.

Proper hand position with the revolver. Also shown is optional finger forward position. The firing thumb may be held high or curled downwards to prevent contact with cylinder release. This is preferable with heavy recoiling loads lest damage to the thumbnail be sustained.

When firing an autoloader, the trigger finger should only be inserted to the point where the first pad is pressing against the trigger.

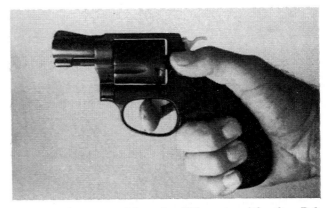

Trigger finger position is different with the DA revolver, as shown. Finger is inserted to the first joint for maximum strength during DA trigger pull.

PRESENTING THE WEAPON FROM THE HOLSTER

1. Stance is assumed, eyes on target (at left).
2. Firing hand obtains a firing grip on gun, weak hand seeks position about 12-14 inches directly in front of abdomen. If autoloader is used, thumb is placed on safety but safety is NOT disengaged. The trigger finger is still outside the trigger guard unless a DA revolver is used.

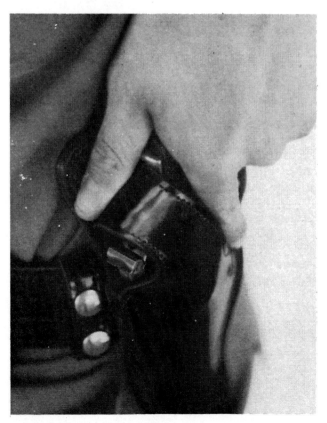

2a. If thumb break holster is used, release of catch is accomplished at this time.

3. Weapon is withdrawn from holster. Thumb safety on auto is still ON, trigger finger is still outside of trigger guard except when DA revolver is used. Eyes are still on the target. If cross-draw holster is used, weapon is rolled under supporting hand and arm in a continuous forward and upward motion.

4. The gun is advanced to a point halfway between the holster and the supporting hand. At this time, the thumb safety of an autoloader is disengaged. The finger is still not on the trigger, eyes are still on the target.

5. The firing and supporting hands intercept and obtain a firing grip. Trigger finger now goes on trigger of auto. Eyes are still on target and the power of the stance is now gained.

6. Under isometric power, the gun is brought to eye level and a sight picture is obtained. You are now ready to fire accurate, controlled shot(s).

PRESENTING THE WEAPON FROM THE HOLSTER (CONCEALED)

Stance is assumed.

As firing hand begins to grasp for butt of gun, little finger sweeps coat aside briskly enough to cause it to swing to the rear. While it is still in motion, firing grip on the weapon is gained. If cross-draw or shoulder holster is used, weak hand sweeps coat away from torso while strong hand seeks firing grip on weapon.

Draw is continued in normal manner.

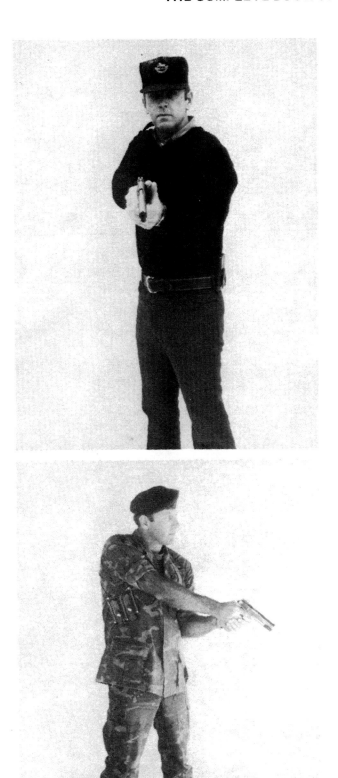

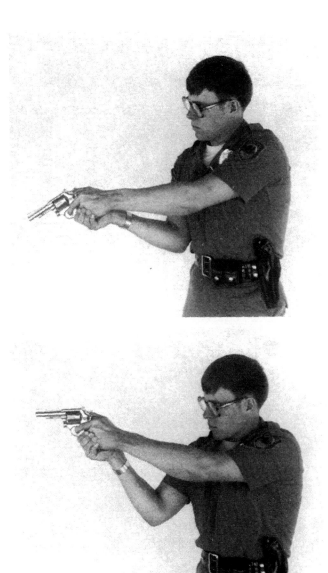

WEAVER READY POSITION

Standard Weaver Stance is assumed, then arms pivoted downwards at the shoulder joint until the gun is down about 45° below horizontal. If the auto pistol is utilized, the trigger finger is kept out of the trigger guard and the thumb safety kept on when the weapon is held in position. During the short time interval as the gun is brought up to eye level to fire, the safety can easily be manipulated and the finger placed on the trigger. Revolvers of the DA type are even easier to work with. The trigger finger may remain on the trigger as the long, heavy DA pull precludes the worry of accidental discharge.

1.

2.

3.

4.

WEAK HAND DRAW

The author recommends against rolling the gun across the front of the torso for safety and control reasons.

5.

6.

SPEED LOAD OF AUTO

1.

2.

3.

4.

STUCK MAGAZINE DURING SPEED LOAD

5.

Little finger of weak hand ejects magazine, fresh magazine is inserted and the procedure continues normally.

TACTICAL RELOAD

1.

2.

3.

4.

5.

6.

7.

8.

SPEED LOAD WITH REVOLVER, WEAPON REMAINING IN FIRING HAND

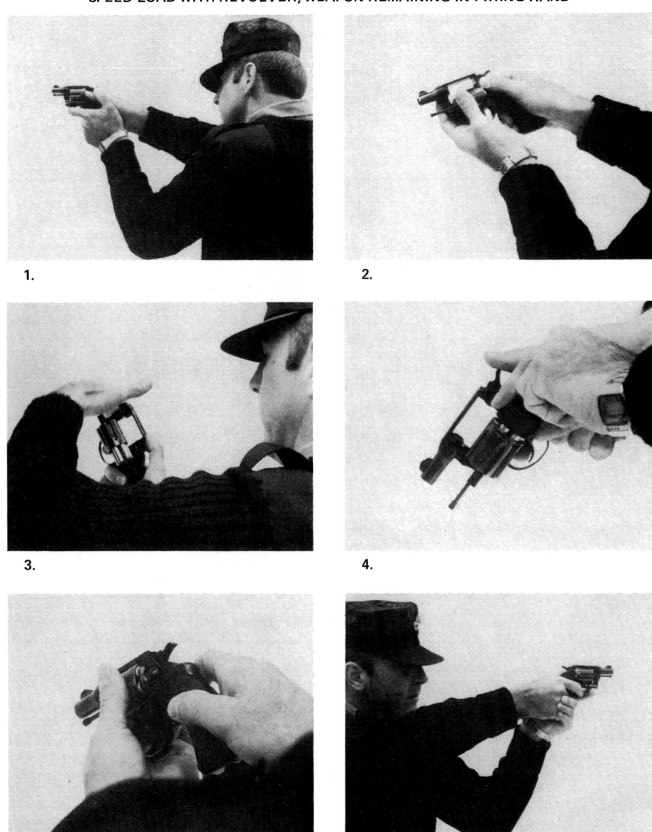

1.

2.

3.

4.

5.

6.

SPEED LOAD WITH REVOLVER, WEAPON CHANGING HANDS
(Author's preference)

1.

3.

Inset: Beware of that one cartridge that fails to properly eject!

2.

TACTICAL RELOAD WITH REVOLVER

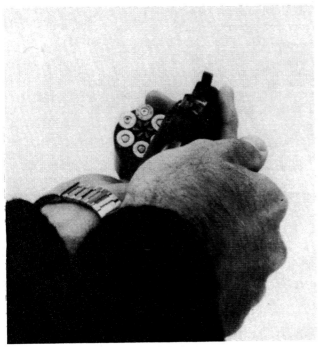

1.

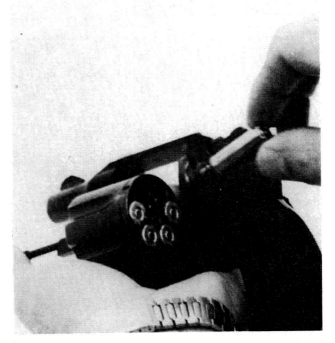

2.

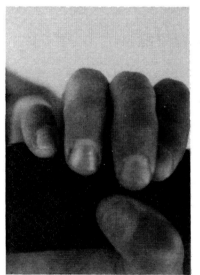
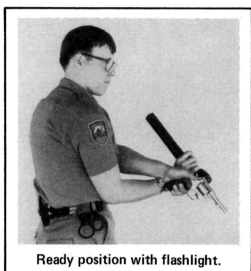
Ready position with flashlight.
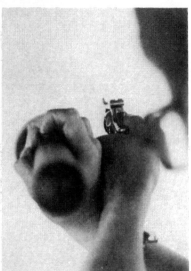

Night shooting technique with a flashlight is only a slightly modified Weaver. This hold provides maximum efficiency and is the best flashlight technique now known.

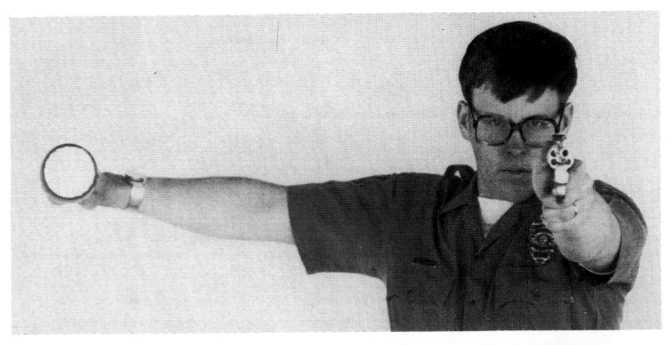

Alternate, and less effective, flashlight techniques are shown above and at right.

MALFUNCTION CLEARANCE DRILL
Failure To Fire — Position 1 Stoppage

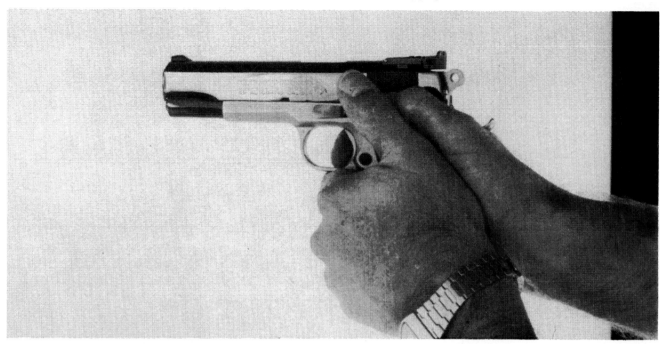

1.

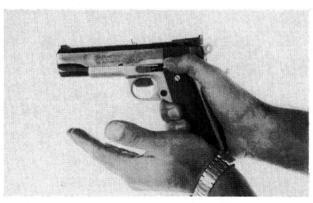

2.

Symptom: Hammer falls, weapon fails to fire. Cure: Tap magazine briskly to insure proper seating, cycle slide once to load new cartridge, and try again.

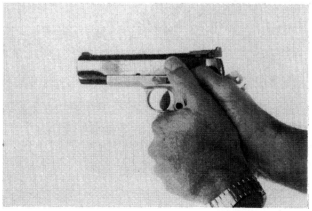

3.

MALFUNCTION CLEARANCE DRILL
Failure To Eject (Stovepipe) — Position 2 Stoppage

1.

2.

3.

4.

Symptom: Case sticking up from ejection port, weapon inoperative. Cure: Weak hand grasps slide with edge of index finger resting against the cartridge case, with tips of fingers and thumb resting as shown. Slide is then briskly withdrawn to the rear, hard enough to throw spent case from weapon and load fresh cartridge into chamber.

MALFUNCTION CLEARANCE DRILL
Feedway Stoppage — Position 3 Stoppage

1.

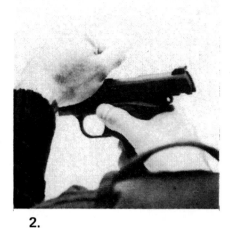

2.

3.

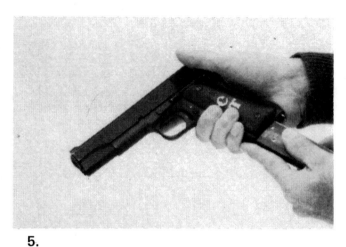

4.

5.

6.

7.

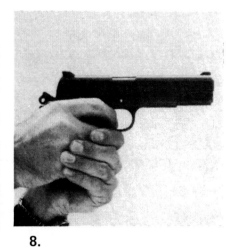

8.

Symptom: Gun inoperative, slide held partially out of battery. Cure: Look into ejection port. If you see brass, lock the slide back, eject the magazine, cycle the slide 2-3 times to clear the mechanism, insert a fresh magazine and briskly ram it home until it locks. Cycle the slide once to load the weapon. You are now ready to fire.

MALFUNCTION CLEARANCE DRILL
Failure To Go Into Battery — Position 4 Stoppage

1.

2.

Symptom: Gun inoperative, slide slightly out of battery. Cure: Brisk slap of supporting hand on rear of slide to fully seat cartridge.

MALFUNCTION CLEARANCE DRILL
Slipped Firing Pin Stop — Position 5 Stoppage

1.

2.

3.

Symptom: Weapon inoperative, slide held back on hammer spur by firing pin stop (bushing) which has slipped down from its location in the rear of the slide. First lock the slide back. Then, with the supporting thumb, briskly press the stop back into place until firing pin pops back into hole. This can be avoided by a strong firing pin spring and/or peening of the firing pin stop to prevent slippage.

90° PIVOT TO THE RIGHT (RESPONSE RIGHT)

90° PIVOT TO THE LEFT (RESPONSE LEFT)

180° TURN (RESPONSE REAR)

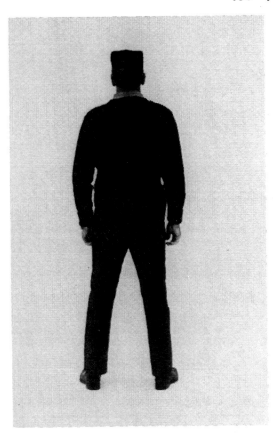

1.   2.

3.   4.

KNEELING POSITION

1.   2.

3.   4.

CHAPMAN ROLLOVER PRONE

1.

2.

3.

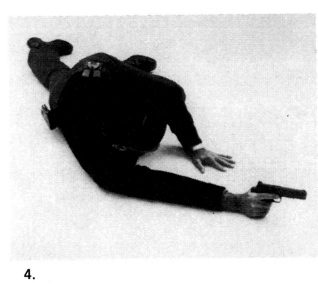

4.

5.

KEITH ROLLBACK POSITION

1.

2.

3.

4.

5.

CLOSE RANGE STEP BACK

WEAK HAND POSITION
The author prefers a straight up weapon attitude over canted position because under stress it requires less thought to properly execute it.

ADVANCED LIVE FIRE DRILL

This program is suggested for those who have completed the Intermediate and/or Advanced Defensive Handgun Course. It does not supplant handling and dry firing exercises which should be practiced 20-30 minutes daily.

All starts are from Condition One, weapon holstered and locked, hands clasped medially, held shoulder high, or at one's sides. It is recommended that the drill be conducted from concealed carry once smoothness is obtained.

1. Warmup Exercises, perform twice. (32 rounds.)
   a. 1 meter, hands held touching shoulders of silhouette target. On command to fire clear target, place two center hits. Time: 1 second.
   b. 3 meters, 2 shots, 1.0 second.
   c. 7 meters, 2 shots, 1.5 seconds.
   d. 10 meters, 2 shots, 2.0 seconds.
   e. 15 meters, 2 shots, 2.5 seconds.
   f. 20 meters, 2 shots, 3.0 seconds.
   g. 25 meters, 2 shots, 3.5 seconds.
   h. 50 meters, 2 shots, 7.0 seconds.

2. Multiples, perform twice. (18 rounds.)
   a. Two (2) silhouette targets, 5 meters, placed 2 meters apart edge to edge. 1 center hit each, 1.2 seconds.
   b. Three silhouette targets, 5 meters, placed 1 meter apart edge to edge. 1 center hit each, 1.5 seconds.
   c. Four silhouette targets, 5 meters, placed 1 meter apart edge to edge. 1 center hit each, 2.0 seconds.

3. Pivots, Turns, perform once each. (15 rounds.)
   a. Five singles, 7 meters. 90° right pivot, 1.2 seconds each.
   b. Five singles, 7 meters, 90° left pivot, 1.2 seconds each.
   c. Five singles, 7 meters, 180° turn, 1.5 seconds each.

4. Failure Drill. Perform three times. 2 shots, down to ready and pause, then 1 center head shot. Time: 1.5 seconds, pause, 1.5 seconds. Range: 7 meters. (9 rounds.)

5. Weak Hand, perform three times. (36 rounds.) Three silhouette targets, 10 meters downrange, spaced two meters apart edge to edge. Draw and fire two rounds at each with the strong hand, reload and switch to weak hand only, fire two more shots at each. Count center hits only. Par time: 9 seconds.

CHAPTER 8

COMBAT HANDGUNNING TACTICS:
The Basics Of Survival

Modern combat handgunning skills have reached a level of efficiency that far surpasses those of history. Indeed there are more Master Class shootists in existence today than ever before — as far as technique is concerned, that is. No, I'm not knocking these men, far from it, because they are very good shots and many of them have critically influenced the very evolution of combat handgunning with their competitive discoveries of winning technique. Yet, most of them lack the most important element of survival skill: *an understanding of tactics.*

If one places himself at the *wrong place at the wrong time*, his survival against an armed opponent hinges upon forces that have nothing whatsoever to do with his own skill. A great shot cannot hit what he does not *see*. The fastest shot in the world will still go to prison if he *fails to properly identify his target* and shoots the wrong person.

It is no secret that under stress people revert to a complete non-intellectual condition known as the *conditioned response*. This, in fact, is the entire reason for training oneself — *to program the proper conditioned responses to the widest possible variety of stimuli.* Almost never is there enough time to intellectually understand the events that take place in a handgun fight because there just isn't time! Annual FBI *Uniform Crime Report* statistics confirm that the average pistol altercation takes place in about 2.8 seconds, with a total expenditure of about 2.7 rounds of ammunition, takes place in dim light, at an average range of 7 *feet.* Last, over 75% of the pistol fights recorded occurred at ranges of less than 7 yards. Interesting, isn't it? What these statistics indicate is that things happen quickly and at extremely close ranges, just out of arm's reach in fact, with handguns.

We have already established that the handgun is by nature a *defensive* weapon. More powerful weapons like the rifle, shotgun and submachine gun perform offensive duty in a far superior fashion to the handgun because the handgun is more difficult to use well, less powerful and lacks range. Yet, these very characteristics make it a superior defensive weapon against unexpected attack. Add to the above the fact that it is light and small, and is thus easily carried and concealed, and the picture is clear.

Use your eyes and ears! When you are inside your world is also inside. Pay attention to what goes on outside the windows and glass doors. The source of danger may have slipped outside as you entered.

Be careful not to drag your torso along walls as you move. Many kinds of clothing emit sufficient noise to be detected and identified. Also avoid scraping your feet on the ground as you move for the same reason — noise.

Never turn your back on anything you haven't checked out first. People can conceal themselves in highly unlikely locations. You cannot afford to assume anything — be CERTAIN!

At the outset we can say that the typical marksmanship problem experienced during a handgun fight is relatively easy and the FBI statistics support that statement totally. This brings us to the point: brilliant marksmanship isn't necessarily a guarantee of survival in a combat situation. But *common sense* goes a long, long way to enhance the odds! In what follows we will explore this largely misunderstood but absolutely critical field in detail, with the hope of providing the reader with maximum understanding of it.

Tactics are not a mixture of voodoo and alchemy, as entirely too many people are under the impression it is. *Tactics merely reflect a crystallization of the various factors of common sense that apply under any given set of circumstances.* Indepth programming of the subconscious mind to react with proper responses to those circumstances is what training is all about.

First I must point out that what will be disclosed herein *is not a guarantee of survival* — only of reduction of danger to controllable levels. It is entirely possible that you can find yourself in an unsurvivable scenario, although statistically it isn't very likely, and no amount of tactical savvy and/or marksmanship skill can save you.

There are six basic parameters of tactical awareness. Adherence to them will do much to minimize your danger and will make your efforts more effective. *Number 1* is to *use your eyes and ears.* Your brain is like the headquarters of a large organization — it must have data to recognize a problem, consider possible courses of action, select a course of action from those possibilities, and, finally, embark upon that course of action. Your

Stay away from corners. Maintain a good, solid ready position as you maneuver. Don't get caught by surprise or in an unready condition.

senses of sight and sound can provide you with invaluable data and, indeed, do just that all of the time. We simply ignore that data, *i.e.*, we look but we don't see and we listen but we don't hear. We do this particularly in an urban environment because we tend to shut out that environment as being basically artificial, which it is. This doesn't mean that elements existing within that environment cannot prey upon us.

When was the last time you paid attention to who might be sitting in that car that just pulled up alongside you at the stoplight? Or, how about the vehicle that appears in your rearview mirror? With urban terrorism on the increase, one cannot afford to ignore what goes on around him for it may indeed prove dangerous, even fatal. The purpose of the handgun is to provide you with the means to regain control of your immediate surroundings when attacked. *If you are not paying attention to those surroundings, how can you do this?*

Along these same lines, the presence of an extraordinary noise might well be an indication of imminent action. The scraping of fabric along a wall in that darkened living room, or the sound of someone dragging their feet along the ground or floor. People tend to do these things when under stress and if you have trained yourself to listen for and recognize them, the element of surprise is on your side instead of your attacker's.

When searching an urban structure or even an outside area, be systematic and thorough in your efforts. Don't let your eyes wander about, drawn by prominent objects or bright colors. Instead, *search in and out on an axis by changing the focus of your eyes along a straight line.* This way even someone not directly in your line of vision will be seen.

No. 2 is *never turn your back on something you haven't checked out first.* Put in another way — don't assume anything, check it out. People can hide in the wildest places if they feel they must, ranging from behind clothes and shoe racks in closets to suspending themselves by their hands and feet from the ceiling of a small room, to crouching on the shelf of a closet. I know of an instance where a burglar was observed entering an urban dwelling by neighbors. The police were notified and a number of officers responded by encircling the house. In the time it took the police to arrive, several minutes, the neighbors stood watch on the place, insuring that the suspect had not left the premises.

When the police searched the house they were unable to find the suspect, even after hours of effort, and finally withdrew under the impression that the suspect had somehow escaped. Fortunately, as the last few officers were making their way back from the interior of the house to the front door, a tiny closet opened, bumping one of the officers as he passed and, from that closet, emerged the burglar! The door to the closet had been opened several times by searching officers, but none had bothered to investigate the inside of the closet further, thinking that the amount of contents of the closet itself precluded the presence of anything as large as a human being. The suspect had been behind some hanging clothes and had remained undetected for almost four hours!

When you are entering a room, make certain that you see *all* of it -- walls and ceiling — before you turn your attention to other things. Remem-

Eyeball view of incorrect way to negotiate a corner. If someone is lurking around the corner junction he will be too close and the time frame too short for you to properly defend yourself. By staying away from corners and stepping out with your weapon at the ready, any assailant must react to you instead of the other way around.

ber that you cannot shoot what you cannot see. But, on the other hand, what you cannot see can indeed attack you with considerable likelihood of success.

The *third rule* of tactics is to *stay away from corners*. Constantly violated by TV and cinema stars, the principle has assumed the proportion in my mind of being one of the most serious facets of combat tactics, perhaps because of my own experiences with it.

I was once in observance of a young infantry officer in Vietnam who had neutralized, we all thought, a North Vietnamese machine gun bunker with a hand grenade after carefully maneuvering to within close range of it. It was common knowledge that most MG teams were made up of two, sometimes even three men, and, from the volume of fire that had been sustained from the bunker it was almost a certainty that there were a number of NVA inside.

Carefully moving along the left side of the now-gutted bunker, the officer, armed with a Thompson submachine gun, made his way to the rear of the structure where the only means of ingress and egress, the rear door, was located.

Avoid potential danger areas as much as possible. These can take the form of a possible attacker armed with an edged or blunt weapon standing out of striking range, or simply a channelized area or possible hiding place. Handle such problems on your terms instead of playing the other guy's game. Example: Would you rather deal with this individual at 8 feet — or at point blank range?

Keep your balance! Don't run unless you are already under fire. Move at a brisk sideways shuffle with your weapon at the ready. Avoid getting your feet crossed while moving.

It was an easy "mop up" maneuver, for there was little danger that anyone inside the bunker had survived the explosion of the hand grenade tossed inside, so the officer was casual in his approach to the left rear corner of the bunker and stepped around it directly at its apex instead of placing himself well away from it and stepping out with his weapon ready.

At the exact instant the officer negotiated the corner an NVA soldier, armed with an AK-47 assault rifle, emerged from the bunker. The U.S. officer sustained three hits from the AK and was able, only through miraculous luck, to kill the NVA with his submachine gun before falling to the ground unconscious from his wounds.

Watch your front sight. If you do, the odds are overwhelming that your shot will hit your attacker somewhere, even if your trigger control isn't as good as it should be. This is not an easy mental task as the eye wants to focus on the source of the excitement. Don't do it!

If you experience a stoppage, take cover to clear it if you can. Don't stand out in the open and fiddle around with your weapon.

This particular incident well illustrates how people get hurt unnecessarily by failing to adhere to common sense tactical principles. The officer should have kept well back from the corner and when he finally exposed himself across the angle projecting from it, he should have done so with his weapon at the ready. Had this been accomplished, the NVA would have been instantly neutralized with no injury whatsoever to the U.S. officer.

This particular incident well illustrates the problem and drove home to me its importance — *because I was that young officer!*

Rule *Number 4* is to *maximize the distance between you and any potential danger area as much as possible.* The closer you are to an attacker, the easier it is for him to get you. Close ranges reduce time frames, giving you less time to react and respond. If the attacker has an edged or blunt weapon he can effectively use it against you. If he has a gun, it will be easier for him to place a hit on you. A man across the room with a knife is no

IF the opportunity presents itself . . . take cover. On automobiles the forward areas adjacent to the tires and engine compartment offer the best resistance to bullets. If available, large trees provide good cover as well as concealment. Know the difference between the two!

problem to someone armed with a firearm. On the other hand, if his location is within a step or two he can bring his weapon into action against you with the possibility of success.

The way to move about when engaged in combative activities is the Weaver Ready position as illustrated on page 92 of this book. Remember not to drag your feet or place your back against a wall as you move — that potential enemy has ears too — and to use your eyes and ears at all times. If you are using a single action auto pistol, don't forget to keep your finger off the trigger and the thumb safety *ON* while "hunting". The gun can be brought to a firing condition as quickly as it can be brought to bear on the target.

Keep your balance — rule No. 5 — don't be caught leaping around. You cannot bring effective fire upon an assailant without keeping yourself under control. Move *briskly* across danger areas but *do not run unless already under fire*. Move in a sideways shuffle, maintaining balance as you go. Keep the direction of your weapon generally in line with where you are looking. *Do not cross your legs.*

Do not fail to understand that the possibility of encountering unarmed or non-hostile personnel exists. For this reason you must never fail to *positively identify your target* before bringing it under fire. This is easily done in the time that it takes to move your weapon from the "ready" to the "point" position. It should also be noted that the law in most states dictates that you must be in fear of your life or immense bodily harm before responding with deadly force. A man armed with a knife or club *standing across the room* may not legally constitute a deadly threat.

The last basic rule is to *watch your front sight*. This one isn't as easy to do as to say because your eyes will be telling your brain to look at the source of excitement. You must fight that tendency and, no matter what, keep your eye focused on the front sight. If you do, you'll hit him, if not — cast your fate to the winds, maybe yes, maybe no. The point is that you do not have to take unnecessary risks.

Other procedures of interest include doorway entry and clearance, malfunction drills and reloading. Reloading and malfunction clearance drills were covered in the preceding chapter and need be discussed here no further.

Doorway entry is a simple procedure that requires only a bit of calm and methodism to execute. First determine which way the door opens — in or out — and *station yourself on the side opposite the hinges*. If the door opens inwards, the hinges will most likely be inside and thus invisible to anyone located outside. If it opens outward, they normally show. In those cases where one may not be able to see the direction which the door travels toward, the doorknob is a good indicator.

Doorway entry when the door swings outward is illustrated above. Remember to keep control of your body and mind. Station yourself on the side opposite the hinges and bring the weapon into a firing position as the door begins to clear.

Doorway entry when door opens inward. Follow the swing of the door inside and insure that it moves all the way to the wall. If anyone is hiding behind it, he must either be struck by it, come out from behind it, or initiate premature action — all of which are to your advantage.

During entry — get through the doorway as quickly as feasible and station yourself off to one side. Sometimes letting your eyes adjust to interior conditions is also a good idea if the situation allows. Don't silhouette yourself against doorways or windows.

The reason for placing yourself on the side opposite the hinges is to allow maximum visibility into the interior as soon as the door begins to swing open, thus providing you with the earliest possible advantage of detection and subsequent reaction.

Once the door is moving, insure that it moves all the way to the wall, in order to discern the presence of anyone behind it. If someone is indeed there, he must either institute action prematurely (you're still outside, remember?), get his face bashed in by the door, or come out. In any case, the advantage remains with you. Then *get inside* and to either side to avoid silhouetting yourself. (This holds true for windows as well.)

If you must reload, take cover to do so unless the need comes in the middle of an exchange of fire. The same applies for clearing malfunctions. Don't stand in the open "fiddling around" with your weapon while bullets fly around you — take cover if you can.

Remember that *just because you are inside, that doesn't mean that your opponent is also inside.*

He may have slipped outside as you entered or moved about after entry and be lurking nearby, perhaps waiting for the opportunity to get a chance at you through a window or plate glass door. When we are inside we tend to pay no attention to this possibility although failure to do so could result in serious injury or even death.

Last, if you do find yourself in a fight, handle it as swiftly and aggressively as possible. When police officers arrive on the scene, insure that your weapon is either put away or held in a non-threatening posture. Police officers are human beings, too, just like you . . . and they have no idea what is going on when they arrive on the scene — only that there has been a call of shots fired or whatever. They have no way of knowing who is who or what has happened and, as a result, they tend to be very careful about endangering themselves, just as you would be. Don't think that they can somehow automatically know that you were the intended victim of the perpetrator because there is no way that they could possibly do so. Be calm and remember that, although the police are not "out to

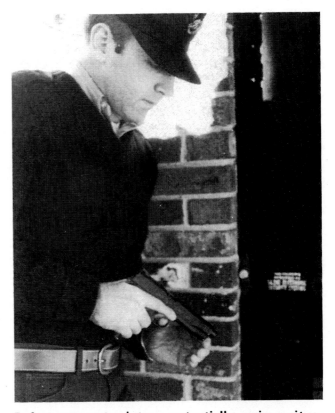

Before you enter into a potentially serious situation make certain that your weapon is in the condition you want it to be in. You are not a fool for checking this, rather a fool if you do not when the opportunity arises.

get you", that statements you make become a matter of official record. Tell the truth correctly and without alteration and do not feel that you are incriminating yourself by having your attorney on the scene where you tell your story. Some authorities go so far as to advise that you call your attorney first . . . then call the police. I personally opine that such a decision rests with the participants involved in the altercation, based upon the circumstances of what happened during its conduct.

Other authorities state that you should automatically prepare yourself to "be sued" by the family of the person you have shot in your own defense. With this I categorically disagree. While it is possible that civil litigation against you could be instituted by the survivors or relatives of the perpetrator of the attack, remember that you were the intended victim and that legal justification in your

use of deadly force in your own defense is also more than adequate defense against civil suit for that act. More often than not, this fact will *prevent* civil suit against you, if anything, because those who are considering the suit will be advised of this by their own attorney. Besides, as an associate of mine recently said, "If it boils right down to it . . . I'd rather be tried by twelve than carried by six." The extreme simplicity and basic honesty of this statement needs no further explanation.

These tips will do much to reduce your personal risk when faced with a tactical situation. Careful adherence to them will make your job much easier, thus freeing your mind to ponder things. "Murphy's Law" and the "KISS" principle both apply to all forms of serious combat and anything you can do to alleviate potential problems before they occur will increase your own survival potential.

ADDENDUM TO CHAPTER 8

Anatomy Of A Tragedy

(What follows is an actual account of a gunfight that took place in 1974 in a large western city. Two police officers and one suspect were involved.

The author has taken the liberty of changing all names to eliminate the possibility of casting aspersions unintentionally upon anyone. The important issue is the event itself, its chronology, and conclusion.

Following the account and accompanying diagrams illustrating the sequence of events is an analysis of the participating officers' actions under stress and how said performances might have been greatly improved by proper indoctrination and training, as well as by the execution of better tactics.

Italics in the text were added by the author for emphasis.)

0920: A disturbance in Municipal Court comes to the attention of Sgt. John Davis and Detective William Brown, who are preparing to testify. A Susan Black tells the officers that Rick White, her former boyfriend, has threatened her and her husband, Johnny Black, with a *knife*. Det. Brown searches White for a weapon, finding none. Sgt. Davis calls the Police Department, requesting a uniformed officer to be assigned the investigation.

0934: Officer Smith, who by coincidence was in front of Municipal Court, is assigned to handle the investigation. Officer Jones, who was in the area, volunteers to assist.

Officers Smith and Jones contacted all parties in Municipal Court. The officers ascertained that Suspect White was cooperative and unarmed. The situation was resolved by White voluntarily leaving Municipal Court since he was not a party to any action there. At this point, White stated that he had no vehicle, that he had taken a bus to the area.

0955: Officer Smith departs from Municipal Court. Shortly after, White departs from the courthouse. Officer Jones remains and continues to talk to the Blacks.

1008: Officer Jones clears from the investigation. Simultaneously, *Officer Smith stops White, driving a Ford Pinto, approximately one block from Municipal Court,* for a right-of-way violation. Officer Smith advises Officer Jones via radio that a stop has been effected at Elm and Main Streets.

1010: Officer Jones joins Officer Smith, parking his motorcycle to the rear of Officer Smith's cycle. Officer Smith informs Officer Jones that he is going to write White a citation. Officer Jones decides to ask White a few additional questions concerning the altercation at Municipal Court.

As Officer Smith was standing to the rear of the driver's door of White's vehicle, and writing a citation, Officer Jones approaches White, who is seated in the driver's seat of the Pinto. Officer Jones tells White he wants to talk with him about the investigation and asks him to step out of the car.

Officer Jones begins to open the driver's door of the Pinto. At this point White, without any previous sign of hostility, attempts to push open the door into Officer Jones, then slams the door shut. A brief struggle ensues; White attempting to hold the door shut while Officer Jones succeeds in opening it by placing his foot against the side of the Pinto and pulling the door open.

White attempts to turn on the ignition key. Almost immediately, Officer Smith appears at Officer Jones' left side, facing into the open door of the Pinto. Officer Smith attempts to get White's hand away from the ignition, while Officer Jones has his arm around White's neck, attempting to extricate him from the vehicle.

White succeeds in starting the Pinto, but it immediately stalls. Suddenly, *White abruptly reaches under the driver's seat with his right hand.* Officer Smith yells: *"Look out, he's got a knife!"* (No knife was ever discovered — author.)

White produces from underneath the bucket seat a .38 caliber revolver and points it at Officer Smith. Officer Jones yells: "Look out!" Both officers jump from the vehicle, Officer Jones begins to move toward the rear of the vehicle at this time. White fires one shot, striking Officer Smith in the right side of the head, the bullet travelling through the brain, exiting from the left side of the head.

Officer Smith falls toward the front of the Pinto, on the left side, in front of the open driver's door.

Officer Jones reaches the left rear of the Pinto, and with weapon in hand, turns to face White.

Officer Jones sees that White is partially out of the vehicle & pointing the gun at him. *Jones fires two shots at White,* but hesitates to fire more, since he believes that Officer Smith has taken cover somewhere toward the front of the Pinto.

In order to keep Officer Smith out of the line of fire, Officer Jones moves toward the right side of the vehicle. While Jones is moving towards this point, he and White exchange fire, White firing three times, *Officer Jones firing approximately 12 rounds* at White from the rear and right rear of the Pinto.

White gets back into the car and attempts to start the vehicle.

Officer Jones observes that White is attempting to flee. He drops the empty magazine from his S&W M59 9mm auto — there had been one round remaining in the chamber — and reloads with a fresh 14 shot magazine. Jones sees that White again points the weapon at him and fires. *Jones fires approximately six rounds at White through the right passenger window of the vehicle.*

White slumps and falls out of the open driver's door of the Pinto onto the street.

Officer Jones runs to the driver's side of the Pinto and sees that White has been hit. He observes White's weapon lying about three feet away from White's outstretched hand, toward the middle of Main Street. Officer Jones still does not see Officer Smith and believes that Smith may be in front of the vehicle.

1011: Officer Jones runs to his cycle and calls for an ambulance.

Jones looks up and sees White, crawling on his hands and knees, attempting to regain possession of his weapon. White recovers the gun, then points it at Jones. Jones fires two rounds at White, hitting him.

Officer Jones runs to the area where White is lying and for the first time observes Officer Smith at the left front of the Pinto. Jones sees that Smith has been wounded and observes a pool of blood by his head.

Officer Jones runs back to his cycle and advises communications that an officer has been shot.

Officer Jones then observes White, again on his hands and knees, *reaching for his weapon.* Jones runs over to White and *kicks the gun out of his hands,* sending it to rest on the double yellow line in the center of Main Street.

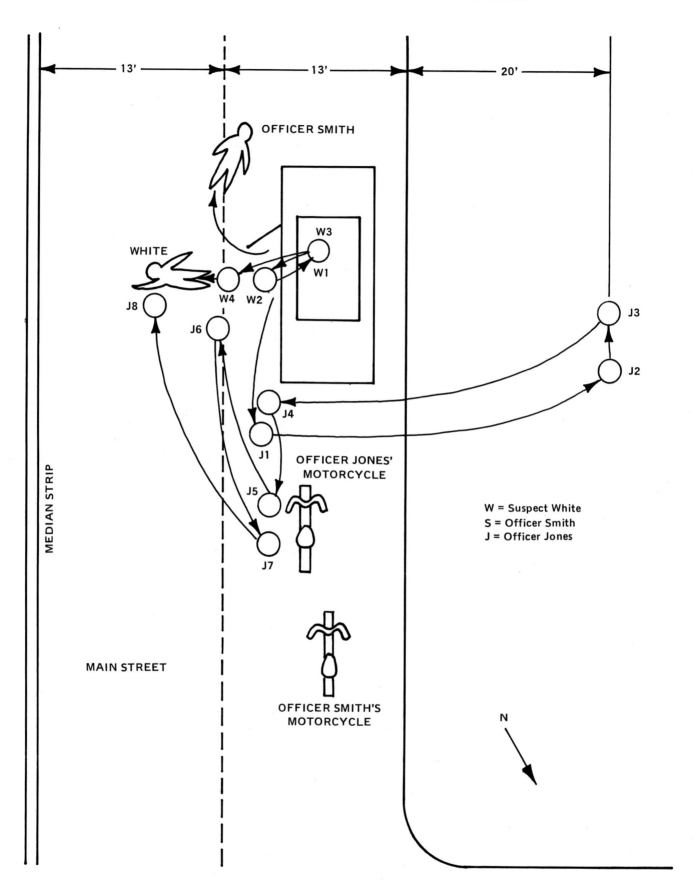

OFFICER SMITH

WHITE

W3

W1

W4 W2

J8

J6

J4

J1

J3

J2

OFFICER JONES'
MOTORCYCLE

J5

J7

W = Suspect White
S = Officer Smith
J = Officer Jones

MEDIAN STRIP

MAIN STREET

OFFICER SMITH'S
MOTORCYCLE

N

LOCATIONS OF PARTICIPANTS IN GUNFIGHT

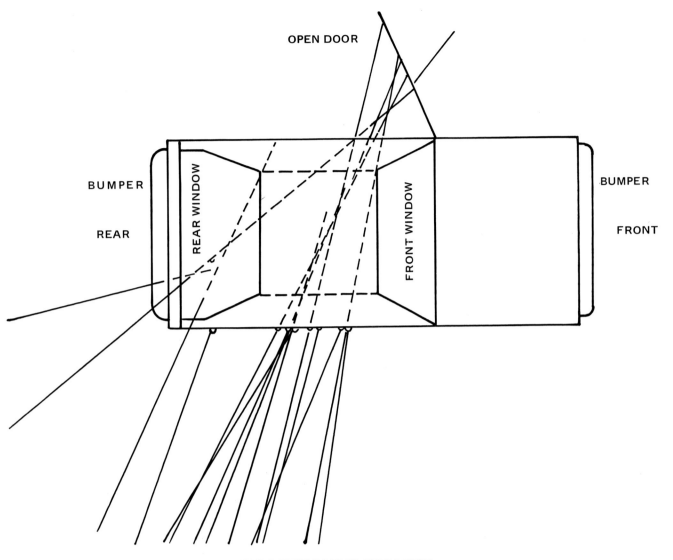

BULLETS' PATHS, TOP VIEW

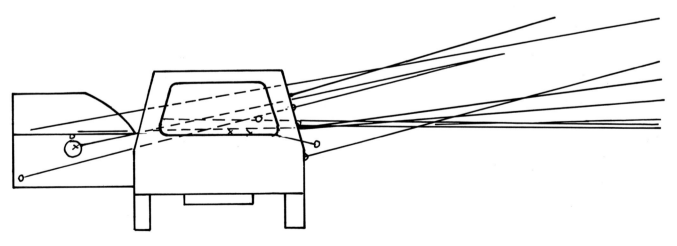

BULLETS' PATHS, REAR VIEW

White collapses. Officer Jones runs to Officer Smith and begins to administer first aid after finding a pulse.

1012: First backup unit arrives at the scene.

1014: Ambulance arrives at the scene and transports Officer Smith to the hospital. Officer Smith is pronounced DOA. *It was noted that Officer Smith's weapon was still in its holster.*

1025: Coroner pronounces White dead at the scene. *Subsequent autopsy revealed that White had fifteen entrance and exit wounds, and had probably been hit 7-8 times.* White had died of a bullet to the aorta.

An inspection of White's weapon disclosed that five rounds had been fired, with a sixth being a misfire.

ANALYSIS OF ACTIONS TAKEN

1. Up to the point where Officer Smith exclaims, "Look out, he's got a knife!" the officers' actions are satisfactory. However, it is interesting to note that Officer Smith's outcry about a knife had to have been the result of a knife being mentioned as the weapon with which White had allegedly threatened his ex-girlfriend's husband at the courthouse. No weapon of that type was found during a search of the suspect at that time or any subsequent time. If Officer Smith's statement of warning about the kind of weapon White was attempting to bring into action had been based upon *observation* instead of arbitrary *assumption* he would have undoubtedly drawn his service weapon as he stepped back from the vehicle, an action which would have done much to save his own life.

2. As White began to step from the vehicle after opening fire and mortally wounding Officer Smith, Officer Jones observed White pointing his weapon at him and fired *two shots* at him with no apparent effect. The range between White and Jones could not have been more than just a few feet, yet both shots failed to bring the altercation to a close. It is unknown if Jones actually *hit* White with these shots, but clearly there is a question here to the effect that better marksmanship might have produced superior results.

3. Officer Jones fired *12 more shots* at White while moving around the rear of and to the right side of the suspect's vehicle, with White returning fire the entire time. Then, *running out of ammunition,* Jones *reloads* and fires *6 more shots* at White, finally wounding him severely enough to at least temporarily incapacitate him. A total of approximately 20 rounds of 9mm Parabellum ammunition have at this point been expended. The danger to bystanders and other non-altercation related personnel within the area was severe and it was most fortunate that no one within that category was injured. Again, more careful marksmanship would have paid much better dividends than did Jones' fusilade of wild gunfire.

4. It is also worth interjecting that it is entirely possible, even probable, that the poor stopping power potential of the 9mm Parabellum cartridge had much to do with the repeated failure of Officer Jones' gunfire to neutralize suspect White. To what degree this is applicable is impossible to ascertain, but the use of a more reliable man-stopping caliber such as .45 ACP, .41 Police, .44 Special or .45 Colt would have ended, with more satisfactory results, the fight much sooner.

SPECIAL NOTE: No criticisms of the officers' character or intelligence are intended. Both were normal male adults, trained in the manner determined by the department by whom they were employed. Their actions under stress were the result of this training and reflect the fact that said training was sadly inadequate insofar as its effect upon the officers' performance under stress was concerned. Analysis of these actions is offered only as an illustration of how important such training can be to survival and to show how typical personnel react and behave during traumatic stress situations.

CHAPTER 9

MENTAL CONDITIONING:
Alertness Minimizes Danger

In an earlier chapter it was stated that one had to be *aware* of his surroundings before he could be expected to possess the ability to *control* them. The police science term for this ability is "situational dominance". The soldier calls it "battlefield savvy".

Whatever one chooses to label it, we are talking about *the ability to at all times be aware of and understand what is taking place within our immediate surroundings.* As long as we can accomplish this, and we are appropriately armed, we can indeed remain in whatever degree of control that we wish to remain of that environment.

Much can be done to make this job easier and the more mental decisiveness that is accomplished *before* the actual fight commences, the better off the protagonist will be. In other words, the more decisions, legal, moral, or tactical, we are able to make before the fight starts, the less we will have to think about during the period of time in which it is actually in progress. In turn, we can then spend more mental energy concentrating on the fundamentals of tactics and/or marksmanship.

While Jeff Cooper was the first to actually set forth in print any attempt at this as applied to individuals, larger organizations, such as the 82nd

Airborne Division, and, later the U.S. Air Force North American Air Defense Command (NORAD) have long operated with their own "DEFCON", that is, *defensive condition*, of readiness to fight. As early as the middle of World War II, the 82nd ABN was known to have used a "color code" of DEFCON, and during the formative years of the Strategic Air Command and NORAD, a similar code was instituted for use as applied to national readiness.

Cooper drew upon the basic principle of this extremely valid principle to set forth four basic mental conditions of readiness, and, once known and understood by the individual, there is no question that those conditions apply as equally to a single human being as they do to an Infantry Division or an entire nation. Regardless of the levels of complexity involved, the principles apply with equal validity.

The first condition is known by the 82nd's assignment of color (and I see no reason to change it, being quite willing to give credit where credit is due) as *Condition GREEN.*

Green connotes a mental state of complete *unawareness* of our surroundings. If attacked in such a state, and are of average mental and physical dexterity, it will take from 2-4 seconds to diagnose the problem, decide upon action, and physically take that action. When the FBI statistics relating to handgun fights are applied to the situation, we find that since the average handgun fight takes place in about 2.7 or 2.8 seconds, our survival potential if caught in Condition GREEN is virtually non-existent, unless our assailant is a complete slob.

It is permissible to be in Condition GREEN only if unconscious, such as when one is literally asleep, as we all must occasionally be. However, when awake, we should never, if we truly care about our own survival if attacked, allow ourselves to dwell in Green.

Instead, and most certainly if we are armed, we live in *Condition YELLOW.* YELLOW has long indicated *caution* and I am certain that the color itself was selected for this reason. And with good purpose, for caution well defines the mental state within which we must function in our chaotic society if we are not to needlessly subject ourselves to attack by the underculture.

In his lectures on the subject, Cooper interjects at this point that *caution* is not *paranoia*, the latter being a mental aberration characterized by visions of persecution. Mental aberrations are fantasies, products of our imaginations. A look at television,

a newspaper, or a short time spent listening to the radio will confirm that what is happening in our world is anything but a product of our imaginations! And this is the difference between the two, is it not? The danger is very real — too real for comfort, in fact — and if caution improves our chances of surviving an unexpected attack then so be it!

When in YELLOW we are not concentrating our mental energies on anything or anyone in particular. Instead we are in a state of "relaxed alert" with no specific point of interest. Included in such a state would be looking at who just pulled up beside you at the intersection, or what kind of car is present in your rearview mirror (and for how long — does it follow you continuously, turn after turn? And if so, who might it be?), etc. This is not paranoia and is interesting because, if for no other reason, one sees so much *more of life* this way!

If a *specific source* of potential danger is detected we should then move into the next highest condition: *Condition ORANGE.* Using the anology of the automobile pulling up alongside us at an intersection, if the person or persons within that vehicle begin behaving curiously or perhaps initiating actions that would possibly be dangerous to our own personal security or safety, we would focus our mental attentions on them. We may not at this point bring our own weapon into readiness or put it in hand, for this would depend upon the specific situation, but we are aware that something is definitely out of the ordinary and that "this just might be it — trouble", and we mentally *begin seeking the best possible position, legal, moral, tactical, from which to deal with the potential problem should it actually materialize as we suspect it might.* Incidentally, much is to be said for the option of avoiding the potential problem by leaving the area if possible. No one is saying that you must unequivocally enter a fight, by any means!

To continue, if the problem continues to escalate into a "possible fight imminent" situation, we move into *Condition RED.* This means that we are ready to fight if necessary and are searching for some action by our adversary that will require our own response. This "mental trigger", as it is called, can be a number of things, among which could be:

1. A weapon of any type.
2. Aggressive actions by the source of my alert.
3. A gun being held by the source of my alert.

MENTAL COLOR CODE

1. GREEN	2. YELLOW	3. ORANGE	4. RED
Unaware Of Surrounding Environment	Relaxed Alert (Unspecified)	Specific Alert (Tactical & Legal Decisions Made)	Fight Imminent! (<u>Mental</u> Trigger)

1. GREEN: A condition of complete unawareness. You will most likely die if confronted by a deadly force situation because of the lack of available time for you to diagnose and solve the technical and tactical problem before you.

2. YELLOW: Relaxed alert, but with no specified focus. You are merely aware that the world is not necessarily a universally friendly place and that at any time something could happen to you.

3. ORANGE: A specific alert condition. You have detected a particular person or thing that is potentially a threat. You will begin to consider tactical and legal ramifications at this point.

4. RED: Fight imminent! Gun may or may not be in hand, but you are ready to employ deadly force if "triggered" to do so by the actions of your source of alert.

The mental trigger may be varied depending upon the circumstances, but common "triggers" are:

    a. A gun held by the source of the alert.

    b. A gun pointed at ME!

    c. A weapon of any type.

    d. Aggressive action by the source of alert.

    4. A gun pointed *at me* by the source of my alert.

To further drive home how important adherence to the "color code" can be and how it can radically affect one's very survival, here is a true story:

A deputy sheriff had arrested a known drug dealer for possession of narcotics during the course of his morning patrol. The suspect was taken to the sheriff's department for questioning and booking.

As the deputy emerged from the sheriff's department building, he observed the suspect, now out of custody on his own recognizance with the assistance of his attorney, leaving the building. Both parties became aware of each other's presence and acknowledged same.

A short time later the deputy was taking his "Code 7" (coffee break) in a nearby diner. He had selected a corner booth which afforded him maximum visibility of the room and was himself seated, drinking a cup of coffee.

The suspect entered the diner, paused at the front door as if searching for someone, saw the deputy, paused again, then moved to the service counter where he seated himself on a swivel stool and ordered coffee, which arrived a few moments later. His arrival on the scene and subsequent actions were observed by the deputy, still seated in the corner booth.

After several minutes passed, the suspect again looked at the deputy, then swivelled his stool sideways, dismounted from it and began walking towards the deputy. The suspect held his cup of coffee in his left hand as he walked. The deputy remained seated in the booth, watching his approach.

As the suspect reached a point at the far edge of the table at which the deputy was seated, he placed his right hand in the pocket of his jacket, a surplus U.S. Army field jacket. The deputy still said and did nothing but observe.

The suspect then drew a .25 caliber auto from his right pocket and emptied it into the deputy's face, killing him almost instantly, and walked from the diner.

When considered in the light of the color code of mental conditioning, the deputy's actions become terribly suspect, for it becomes painfully clear that his death was, as are those of most law enforcement officers killed in the line of duty, completely unnecessary — a tragedy, if you will.

When the suspect for the second time encountered the deputy, should he not have mentally "filed it away" as being a possible coincidence, but nonetheless focused his concentrations upon the suspect "just in case"? A police officer should be, by virtue of his job if for no other reason, in no condition of mental readiness less than YELLOW. When the suspect entered the diner, observed the officer, paused, and then seated himself at the service counter, the deputy clearly should have placed himself in Condition ORANGE and begun considering possible courses of action.

When the suspect again looked at the officer, then dismounted from the stool and began walking towards him, should the officer have remained seated? Or could he have removed himself from the booth, assumed a position from which he could legally and tactically defend himself and challenged the suspect with "Hold it right there, Bill . . . what can I do for *you*?" or something to that effect? Perhaps the display of obvious readiness would have discouraged the suspect from attempting any aggressive action, for with the intended victim obviously ready to respond, and with witnesses present on the scene, his chances of successful execution would have been minimal at best. *Maybe nothing at all would have happened if the deputy had done what was outlined above!*

Most certainly when the suspect continued to walk toward the seated deputy, something should have been done to alter the possible direction of events. Had the deputy been out of the booth, possibly now with his weapon ready, any action instituted by the suspect would have been foolish, and, if instituted anyway, would have resulted in the suspect, instead of the officer, being injured.

If the suspect continued to walk towards the officer after being challenged, Condition RED would have been in order. What might have happened after that is anyone's guess, but it is easy to see that the chain of events need not have been as it actually occurred — with the deputy being killed needlessly in the process. It could have been — and should have been — the other way around.

As you can see, the color code is an important and decisive part of "battlefield savvy". Adherence to it, in conjunction with proper tactical execution and good technique of weapon handling, can if not eliminate entirely, reduce drastically your danger when caught in a deadly force defensive situation.

CHAPTER 10
TRAINING & COMPETITION

No one can become proficient with a firearm or any other kind of weaponry without serious continuous practice. However, this does *not* mean unequivocally that you must be spending hours daily on the firing range burning gunpowder. In fact, only *minimal* time need be spent actually firing your handgun, this being required to confirm your subconscious mind, nerves and muscles that everything your *dry practice* has programmed into you is being executed properly. Live work confirms and reconfirms on a continuing basis that you are familiar enough with the elements absent

from dry practice — noise & recoil — that they will not act as a negative factor when you actually fire your defensive handgun for real.

This was confirmed several years ago by former IPSC World Champion David Westerhout, who by requirement also spent considerable time in the Rhodesian armed forces, as did every other able-bodied male in that country. David was concerned with handgun training, not surprisingly, and discovered that sanctions against his country had caused ammunition to be a prime shortage. In response to this, he attempted to ascertain if

Man-against-man competition is a good simulator of combative stress, possibly the best available. If careful attention is paid to the course of fire used, a great deal of benefit can be derived from such activities.

troops could achieve a reasonable level of proficiency without ever actually firing their handguns until qualifications day when they fired for the record. The result of David's experiments was that the group he trained using totally *dry* techniques shot slightly *higher* scores than did the group who had been trained in the conventional live-fire manner.

Upon examination, it is surprising that no one ever thought of this before because combat handgunning, like many other semi-athletic activities, is largely a *motor reflex*, and, since motor reflexes are enhanced by *repetition*, there is no reason whatsoever why one could not attain a fairly high level of reactive skill (conditioned response) derived solely from dry practice of basic movements.

It is therefore required that, depending upon the degree of skill you wish to attain, you spend only a relatively small portion of your overall practice effort on live fire. Current economics being what they are (standard .38 Specials cost about $11.00 per box of 50 as of this writing), dry practice is an added benefit! Further financial savings may be derived by indulging in the hobby of handloading one's own practice ammunition. But a word to the wise from one who knows: *Don't carry handloads in your defensive handgun for actual combative use.* Use instead the best factory ammunition that you can buy in the load you select. We're talking about shooting that weapon to save your own life, remember? And it is very important that we always keep our perspective on this fact.

The building of basic fundamental skills is the most important facet of training. Don't let anyone fool you . . . it is these fundamentals that save your life!

Moving target training is fun, but not as important as a number of other categories of emphasis. Targets rarely move in real life the way they do on a lateral track and the law in most states precludes shooting fleeing felons, etc.

Practical shooting competition is highly useful as a training tool when realistic courses of fire based upon relevancy to reality are employed. Here the shooter must get up from bed to engage targets after scooping up his weapon from a simulated nightstand. I thought the Teddy Bear was a nice touch, too!

One of the most serious problems with "Practical Shooting" competitions is that quite often equal emphasis is placed upon athletic ability as well as shooting skills. This is an error and is totally unrealistic if competition is to be used as a training instrument. As often said by several professionals in the field: "I carry a pistol so I don't have to run!"

Maximum emphasis should be placed upon use of the handgun from concealed carry. Not as easy as it looks, this is by far the normal mode of handgun carry.

Since handgun action rarely takes place past 15 meters maximum, no emphasis should be placed upon long range shooting. Instead dwell upon the closer ranges and on realistic solution of tactical problems.

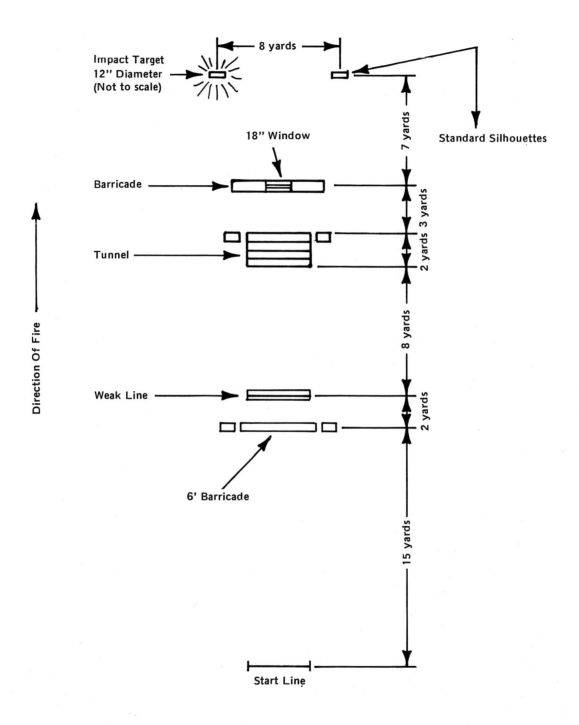

Impact Target 12" Diameter (Not to scale)

8 yards

Standard Silhouettes

18" Window

7 yards

Barricade

2 yards   3 yards

Tunnel

8 yards

Weak Line

Direction Of Fire

2 yards

6' Barricade

15 yards

Start Line

Caution should be exercised in the use of irrelevant courses of fire when survival training is the prime objective of participation. The handgun is intended as a defensive weapon and all efforts towards serious training must reflect this philosophy. Unfortunately, so called "practical" handgun competition fails to recognize this critical requirement most of the time, pursuing instead a course of intense physical locomotion that puts more emphasis upon physical rather than shooting skills and ignores tactics completely. "Practical" competition SHOULD be just what the name says it is.

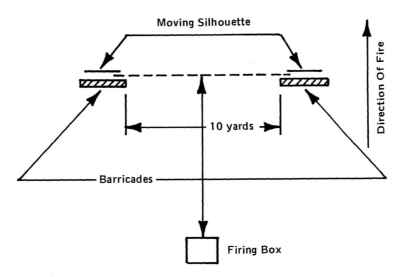

The layout above is an example of a useful competitive course of fire. Although participants in handgun fights rarely run back and forth laterally,

In the technique section of this book, the basic motions of handling your weapon are covered: a good solid Weaver Stance, presenting the weapon to the target from either the Combat Ready or Holstered position, pivots and turns, reloading (tactical and speed), malfunction clearance drills and loading/unloading/checking your weapon.

Complex and unrealistic courses of fire require the shooter to practice the exact problem in advance in order to be competitive. Since this cannot possibly be accomplished with street encounters, etc., such courses are poor means of combat training. Here the best shot in the world, Ross Seyfried, demonstrates his many competitive skills during the 1979 IPSC World Championships in South Africa.

the basic idea of training shooters in the fundamentals of lead and swing is a good idea as well as being great fun!

Devoted effort to dry practicing these will take you quite far in building your skill. At the outset, about an hour per evening in the isolation of your home will provide you with maximum learning absorption. After about a week, taper this down to 30 minutes of concerned effort per evening and maintain this schedule for the next three weeks.

During the first week of dry practice, concentrate upon proper learning of the basic skills with no emphasis upon speed. Speed is the natural by-product of the absence of the waste of motion, so concentrate instead on becoming *smooth* and fluid in your execution of the motions involved. After a couple of practice sessions, there is a natural tendency to begin attempting to strive for increased speed. I urge you to resist this tendency and continue to expend your energies in achieving smoothness. Only after the basic motions and maneuvers are thoroughly mastered should one begin striving for increased speed. To do so only results in disappointment which in turn slows down the learning process by damaging one's attitude.

When you finally do reach the point where you feel ready to attempt increases in speed of execution, an associate must be recruited for stop watch operation and your times should be recorded for comparison purposes so you can gauge your progress. An even better idea is to purchase a self-contained timing apparatus built by T-Enterprises of Houston, Texas. This handy little device precludes the need for a second party to be involved in your dry (or live) practice sessions and this obviously makes the act of actually practicing much easier.

Shooting bowling pins is great fun also, but is in no way preparative for combat situations. Often billed as being "combat" matches, such shooting must be viewed with skepticism as a training method.

Special events for prizes are also often misunderstood as being tactical exercises. Here shooter is attempting to empty two .38 Special snubbies in one target in 3.0 seconds.

The timing unit features an earplug assembly and adjustable time-frame settings. Using it, you can determine how your performance compares against the dry/live practice drills included in this chapter. Cost of the unit is about $100.00, but it is worth every cent in convenience!

Live fire practice should at first be scheduled weekly with a strict limit on the quantity of ammunition expended (again refer to Basic Live Fire Drill described on page 80). Shooting *too much* live ammunition does nothing to improve your skill. As with all other learning activities, there is a point where the mind, and sometimes the body as well, simply cannot absorb more data. This is caused by fatigue and any attempt to force matters normally results in less than satisfactory

The great Ray Chapman, dean of the competitive shooting fraternity. If you want to learn how to shoot in IPSC matches, Ray is your man.

Since the average handgun engagement range is 7 FEET, maximum emphasis should be placed upon possible action at close range, Here the author demonstrates a "step back" from simulated felon followed by two quick shots to the chest . . . in 1.0 second!

achievement. In turn that same lack of achievement of a self-set goal fosters disappointment and anger, neither of which is a constructive mental condition as far as learning is concerned. No one expects you at first to be able to perform all of the motions listed on the drill sheet to perfection and the key to finally reaching the point where you can say you have mastered them is *intelligent, consciencious, sustained* practice. So, don't try to do too much too quickly.

As the skills listed on the Basic Drill sheet become easily performed, switch to the Advanced Drill and work with the time-frames listed therein until you can perform all of the motions listed in a satisfactory manner. Once accomplished, you can say that you can handle any basic combative maneuver with no problem.

Shooting from a moving vehicle is difficult and unlikely to be required in typical situations due to tactical and sometimes legal considerations, but should be a part of the serious handgunner's training to some degree.

In situations where space prohibits gaining standoff distance from an attacker, belt level shooting is useful. Shown is the so-called "Speed Rock" with two center chest hits in 1.0 seconds. Care must be taken to keep weapon out of arm's reach of target lest one lose custody or shooting control of his weapon.

Since the other half of survival in a life and death situation is mental it is an excellent idea to consider the potential tactical principles as listed in Chapter 8 in your own home and/or business. Insure that your weapon is empty and go ahead — clear your house or business when there is no one around. You will find that it is an illuminating experience to say the least. Pay particular attention to your heartbeat and respiration after you finish. If you are really taking your practice seriously both will be quite high! Now think of what it must be like to do it for *real* . . . stress is what it is called, and the more simulation of it you can experience, the better off you will be. It is better to sweat a little now than to go to pieces during an actual fight. Anyone who says otherwise is a fool.

Another good idea is to discuss possible signals, etc., with your wife and family. Standard drills in case of a hostage situation, burglary, or armed

Indoor reaction ranges, where available, are superb instruments as long as they are not made into competitive "track meets", as some competitors call them, in which the shooter must race through a structure without regard to tactics or common sense.

Outdoor reaction ranges such as this "jungle lane" are good training tools and a tremendous amount of fun as well. Again, don't turn it into a "track meet", or all value is lost.

robbery attempt make things safer and a lot easier on all concerned. Sure, call the police if you can, but *if you cannot, guess who will have to handle the problem — you!* And, after all, who must be ultimately responsible for the safety of you and your family? Right — *you*. It's really more common sense than anything else, isn't it?

So called "practical" handgun competition, as characterized by the International Practical Shooting Confederation (IPSC) or the "Police Combat" type shooting clubs, is limited in value as a training tool because both have lost sight of the basic purpose of the handgun as it is used in combat. This loss of principle is not uncommon in many activities that began as simulations of real situations and is caused by unqualified personnel contributing courses of fire to an overall competitive shooting program. The result of both the IPSC program and the PPC course is that little attention is paid to the actual conditions under which the defensive handgun is employed and although both shooting disciplines are great *fun*, neither can withstand the revelations of the "cold light of day". The handgun is a defensive arm and running about the countryside, hanging from ropes and hooks, walking narrow planks, climbing walls and emphasizing speed reloading hardly epitomize reality. Moreover, the use of special (non-service) guns, target ammunition, speed holsters and other non-service accessories further undermines the credibility of both IPSC and PPC activities. Enough data exists for any qualified person to readily see why both of these types of shooting fail to satisfactorily prepare one for a fight. The simple fact of the matter is that both require a participant to use guns, accessories and tactics that are not only unheard of, but in some cases *suicidal*, if they hope to have any chance of winning the competition. When this becomes obvious to even the casual observer, as it has at all of the major IPSC matches, for example, it is time to call things what they are . . . Practical it ain't, folks!

If I seem over-critical of IPSC, I apologize, but the business of saving lives is *serious*. And the egotism of many of the unqualified people involved in IPSC appears to preclude them from perceiving the deviation from reality that has been suffered by their organization.

As a once-prominent IPSC competitor myself, I regard this situation as being most unfortunate and fought incessantly to prevent it from happening, as did my associate Ken Hackathorn. Unfortunately our efforts were ignored and the slide into unreality continued to its present point.

Over-emphasis on athletics is the bane of the true combat shooter. Available statistics cannot be ignored in course design if realistic defensive training is the primary object of the exercise. Moreover, there is no reason why competition and realistic training cannot overlap and mix benefit with fun.

THE "J" LADDER

Man-against-man competition is a good substitute for the actual stress of combat. If an intelligent course of fire is utilized it can help a great deal in developing survival shooting skills.

THE FLYING M

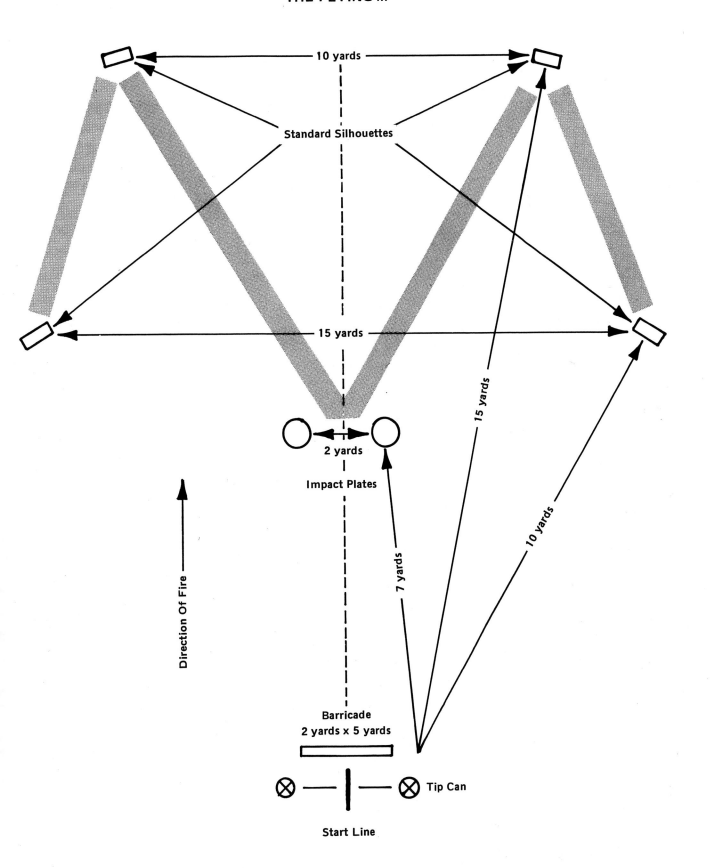

10 yards

Standard Silhouettes

15 yards

15 yards

7 yards

10 yards

2 yards

Impact Plates

Direction Of Fire

Barricade
2 yards x 5 yards

Tip Can

Start Line

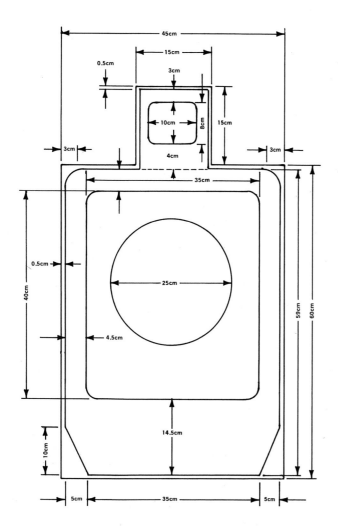
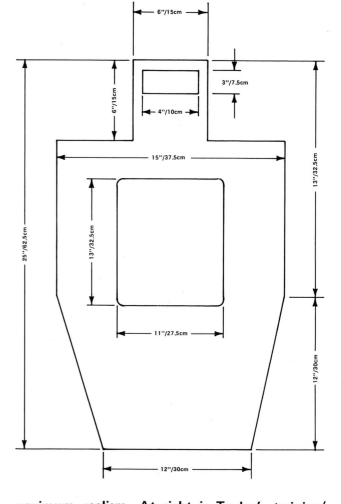

Sample competitive target (L) IPSC Milpark type as designed by author Taylor, Alec DuPlessis of Rhodesia and Vidar Nakling of Norway. Taylor's criticism of target is that it is too wide and should be reduced in width by about 4" for maximum realism. At right is Taylor's training/competition target, which provides more attention to placing speed and accuracy in proper balance with layout of vital organs.

Competition, provided relevant courses of fire are utilized, can be an extremely useful training and evaluation tool — and everyone can have fun at the same time. There is no reason whatever for the separation of the two. Thus, when considering participation in competitive shooting activities, be careful. Choose only those courses of fire that provide a reasonable degree of relevancy or relationship to real life in which to engage.

Perhaps one day realism will triumph over "gamesmanship", but until this actually happens, a certain degree of caution and skepticism toward most so called "practical" competition must be exhibited.

Glossary

Handgun Nomenclature

Arms Manufacturers And Importers

Accessories — Where To Find Them

Handgun Related Publications

Military Handguns Of The World

Custom Pistolsmiths: Men Who Understand
Your Combat Handgun

Ammo Data: .45 ACP & 9mm Parabellum

Pro-Gun Editorial

REFERENCE
SECTION

GLOSSARY: Terminologies & Definitions

ACTION: *Breech mechanism of a gun by which it is loaded and unloaded.*

AIR SPACE: *Space in a loaded cartridge not occupied by propellant powder.*

ANVIL: *In a primer or cartridge case, a fixed point against which the priming mixture is compressed, and thereby detonated, by the action of the firing pin.*

BALL: *Early term for "bullet" — still used in military descriptions of issue ammunition.*

BALLISTICS: *The science of projectiles in motion.*

Cartridge <u>Case.</u> Often erroneously termed a "shell".

BARREL: *A tube through which the projectile of a firearm is accelerated into flight. The standard length of handgun barrels varies from two to as long as fourteen inches. Combat handguns normally feature barrels of less than 8-3/8 inches.*

BLOW BACK: *A type of semi-automatic action in which the breech is not locked shut, but rather*

Cartridge <u>Head.</u>

held shut by spring tension and inertia, and simply blown open on recoil. It is suitable only for low powered cartridges. It is universal in auto pistols chambering the .22 rimfire cartridge.

BLACK POWDER: *A mixture of charcoal, sulphur and potassium nitrate used as a propellant. Produces much smoke and fouling when burned.*

BORE: *The interior surface, or space, of the barrel.*

Bullet. This example is a semi-wadcutter (SWC) configuration.

Hollow Point Bullet. Often erroneously called a "dum-dum".

BULLET: *A single projectile launched from a small arm. A contemporary error is the use of the term "bullet" for "cartridge".*

BULLET JACKET: *A capsular covering of metal harder than lead and softer than steel which encloses a bullet's core, intended to take and hold rifling at velocities that would strip lead.*

BORE DIAMETER: *In rifled arms, the diametrical measurement between tops of the lands.*

BREECH BOLT: *The part of a breech that resists the rearward force of the combustion that occurs when a cartridge is fired.*

BUTT: *That part of a handgun which is grasped by the firing hand, composed of the lower rear portion of the frame together with the stocks.*

BULLET MOULD: *Metallic device with a cavity or cavities into which molten lead is poured and allowed to harden into projectiles.*

CALIBER: *The diameter of the bore, measured, in small arms, to the depth of the rifling grooves. Caliber is typically expressed in hundredths or thousandths of an inch, or in millimeters.*

CANNELURE: *Circumferential groove(s) around a bullet or cartridge case. In the latter, refers to the extractor groove; in lead bullets, the lubrication grooves; in jacketed bullets, the expansion point and/or where the cartridge case is crimped.*

CARTRIDGE: *A complete round of ammunition, made up of a cartridge case, primer, propellant powder and bullet.*

Round Nose (RN) bullet design. Can be lead or jacketed.

Cartridge. The entire package of bullet, case, primer and powder.

Left: Metal Piercing bullet, usually truncated and hard jacketed to enhance penetration effect. Center: Soft Point Bullet, also erroneously termed "dum-dum". Right: Semi-wadcutter Bullet. This example is a lead hollow point.

Specialty Ammunition. L to R: Glaser Safety Slug (prefragmented bullet), Tracer and Metal Piercing (KTW).

CARTRIDGE CASE: *The container in which the bullet, propellant powder and primer are housed. Often referred to as "brass" or as being an "empty".*

CF: *Centerfire. Those cartridges which are ignited by means of a separate and replacable primer.*

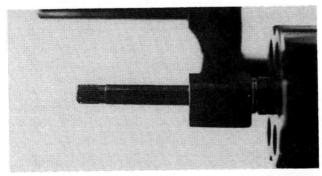

Ejector Rod. Found on all modern double action revolvers.

Ventilated Rib. For cooling barrel more quickly.

CHAMBER: *That portion of the bore, at the breech, formed to accept the cartridge.*

CLIP: *A device, usually of metal, used to hold several cartridges together to facilitate packaging or loading. A "stripper clip" is one from which cartridges are forced by hand into the magazine.* A magazine is not a clip!

CHRONOGRAPH: *An instrument which measures the velocity at which a projectile travels.*

CORDITE: *A nitroglycerine smokeless propellant powder used mainly in England.*

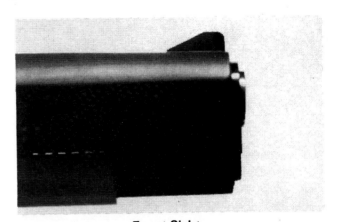

Front Sight.

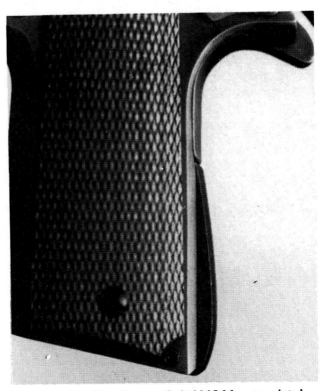

Mainspring Housing on Colt M1911 auto pistol.

COCK: *Originally a noun denoting the swinging arm of a flintlock that scraped the flint against the frizzen. Now a verb describing the act of forcing the hammer or striker against the mainspring to prepare for firing.*

CRIMP: *The bending inward of the case mouth perimeter, in order to grip and hold the bullet.*

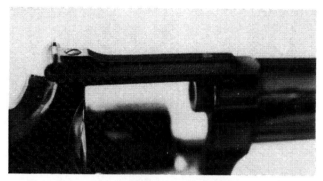

Top Strap on modern double-action revolver.

CYLINDER: *In a revolver, a cartridge container that rotates around an axis parallel to and below the barrel. Each time the weapon is cocked a chamber containing a cartridge is brought into line with the barrel.*

DRIFT: *The bullet's movement to right or left, away from the line of the bore, caused by the bullet's rotation or spin.*

DOUBLE-ACTION: *A firing system which permits a firearm to be fired in two ways, either from a cocked or uncocked condition. Today, the term usually denotes the trigger-cocking mode of revolver operation.*

Ejection of spent cartridges.

Ratchet.

Revolver. This specimen sports a 2 inch (snubby) barrel.

DISCONNECTOR: *Any device that takes part of a mechanism out of action with another so as to render that mechanism inoperative. In handguns, the term refers to the component that acts to disconnect the trigger mechanism until the breech is completely shut, thus preventing premature discharge.*

EJECTOR: *The device at the breech or within the action that knocks the fired case from the gun.*

ENERGY: *In projectiles, the amount of work done, at given ranges, as expressed in foot-pounds. Also known as "kinetic energy". Obtained by multiplying the mass of a moving object times one-half the square of its velocity. Energy is one form of measuring the so-called "power" of a firearm. It is, however, not the only means.*

Self-loading Pistol. Often called an "automatic".

EROSION: *The gradual wearing away of rifling in the barrel by combustion gas.*

EXTRACTOR: *The device that withdraws the fired case from the chamber.*

FIREARM: *A weapon that employs internal combustion to initiate the flight of its missile.*

FIRING PIN: *A pin which, when actuated by the trigger, strikes the primer of the cartridge, thus detonating it and causing the bullet to begin its movement through the bore as the result of expansion of propellant gases ignited.*

FLASH GAP: *The space between the forward edge of the cylinder and the rear end of the barrel in a revolver.*

FOLLOWER: *A metal platform in a magazine that pushes the cartridges upward for feeding into the chamber.*

FULL COCK: *The condition of the piece when the mainspring is fully compressed.*

GAS CHECK: *A cup, usually of copper, used at the base of a lead bullet to protect it from hot powder gases.*

GAS OPERATION: *In small arms, an automatic or semi-automatic action in which the barrel and breechblock are positively locked together, and stationary, during discharge, and in which a portion of combustion gas is diverted far enough to permit combustion pressure to drop, and used to unlock the breech and operate the action.*

Grip Safety.

Left: Muzzle. Right: Barrel bushing for auto pistol.

Ejection Port.

GILDING METAL: *A copper-zinc alloy used as a bullet jacket.*

GROOVES: *Spiral cuts in a bore which cause the bullet to spin as it travels down the bore.*

GROOVE DIAMETER: *In rifled arms, the diametrical measurement between bottoms of grooves.*

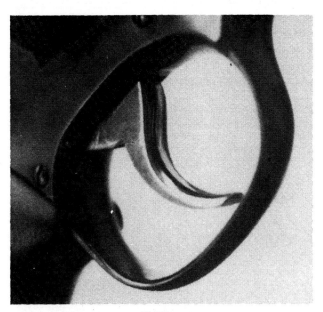

Trigger.

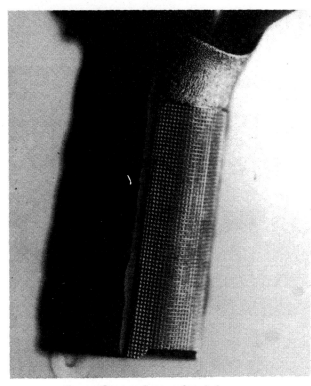

Front Strap. Auto pistol shown.

Half-moon clip for M1917 S&W and Colt revolvers.

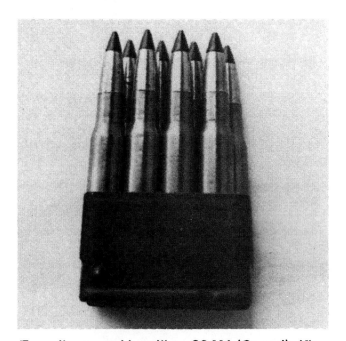

True clip, as used in caliber .30 M1 (Garand) rifle.

GRIP: *The method of placing the hands upon the piece,* not *the wooden or plastic portion of a pistol butt.*

GRIP SAFETY: *A device designed to prevent a pistol from firing unless it is properly gripped in the firing hand.*

GROUP: *The number of shots fired into a target, usually with one sight setting.*

GUN: *Loosely stated, any firearm. Correctly stated, a flat-trajectory cannon, as opposed to a howitzer, mortar, or shotgun.*

HAMMER: *A part of the action actuated by the trigger. The hammer drives the firing pin against the primer, thus igniting the cartridge powder charge.*

HANDGUN: *A small firearm with a short barrel and no buttstock which can be worn upon the person. It may be fired with one hand but it is more effectively used with two.*

HANG-FIRE: *An abnormal delay in cartridge ignition after the primer is struck by the firing pin.*

HP: *Abbreviation for "hollow point" — a form of expanding bullet.*

Stocks, revolver (L) and auto (R) styles.

LOAD: *A specific cartridge or the exact specifications for a cartridge. Also the act of putting a complete cartridge into the firing chamber of a firearm. A piece with an empty chamber and a loaded magazine in place is not actually "loaded".*

LOCKED BREECH: *A firearm action in which the breech is positively and mechanically locked during firing.*

Barrel. At top is a 2 inch version while the lower barrel is 8-3/8 inch.

HEADSPACE: *For rimmed cartridges, the distance from the face of the breechblock to the barrel seat for the forward surface of the case rim. For a rimless cartridge, the distance from the face of the breechblock to a predetermined point on the shoulder of the chamber.*

HOPLOPHOBIA: *Phrase made popular by handgun expert Jeff Cooper. Used to denote a mental aberration characterizing an inordinate fear of weapons.*

LANDS: *That portion of the bore remaining after the rifling or grooves have been cut.*

LEADING: *Lead deposited on bore surfaces by bullets passing through.*

Holster.

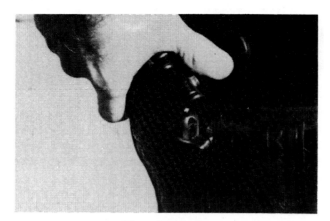

Thumb Break.

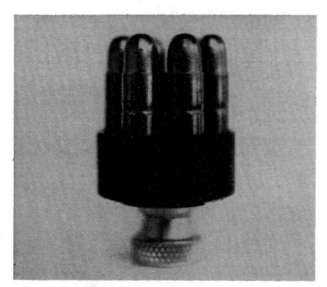

Speed Loader for revolver.

Speed Loader Pouch.

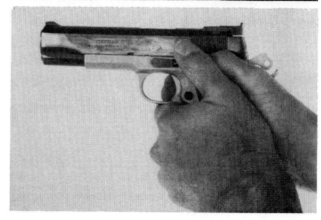

Grip, one-hand, and two-hand Weaver style shown with revolver and auto.

MAGAZINE: *Device or reservoir to hold extra cartridges, usually residing within the firearm it-self. A magazine always incorporates a feeding (follower) spring whereas a clip does not. A magazine is not a clip.*

M.C.: *Metal Case. A form of bullet completely covered with gilding metal.*

Spare magazine carrier for auto.

MIDRANGE: *Usually used in connection with trajectory, referring to a point midway between muzzle and target.*

MRT: *Midrange trajectory.*

MISFIRE: *A cartridge that does not ignite when struck by the firing pin.*

MAGNUM: *A contemporary term for a cartridge or a handgun firing said cartridge, which is intended to develop higher projectile velocities and pressures than typical of the breed. In actuality, the term is used to describe a very large container of champagne!*

Hammer drop safety.

MAINSPRING: *The spring which drives the firing mechanism of a firearm. Not necessarily the largest spring in a firearm.*

MOMENTUM: *The amount of motion of a moving body. The figure is obtained by multiplying the mass of a projectile times its velocity. Momentum is a more satisfactory means of measuring the power of a handgun.*

MUSHROOM: *The capacity of certain bullets to expand on or after impact.*

Thumb safety, extended type, shown on Browning P-35 Hi-Power 9mm auto.

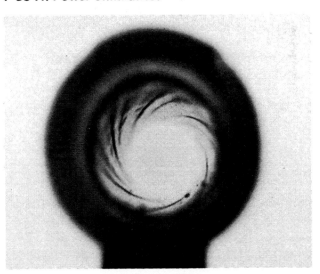

Bore, includes rifling lands and grooves.

MUZZLE: *End of barrel opposite to breech, from which the bullet exits into free flight when the weapon is fired.*

M.E.: *Connotates "Muzzle Energy".*

M.V.: *Denotes "Muzzle Velocity".*

PRESSURE: *The gas pressure generated in a cartridge on its being fired, usually expressed in pounds-per-square-inch, or copper-units (CUPS).*

Submachine Gun. A machine pistol is not a sub-machine gun.

PIECE: *Any small arm. Derived from "piece of ordnance".*

PISTOL: *Loosely stated, any handgun. Correctly stated, a self-loading handgun.*

POWER: *In small arms, the force expended by a cartridge when fired in a specific weapon. Often measured by comparisons of kinetic energy, but more correctly expressed by comparisons of momentum.*

PRIMER: *The small cup containing a detonating mixture which is seated in a recess in the base of the case. In a rimfire, a similar mixture is seated in the rim of the case.*

RANGE: *The distance to which a missile is thrown. In small arms "maximum range" is the absolute distance a bullet will travel before landing. In the practical sense, "maximum range" denotes how far away one can effectively hit his opponent with a shot or shots fired. Thus the term has more to do with marksmanship than technology.*

RECOIL: *Newton's Law — "For every action, there is an equal but opposite reaction." Also known as "kick". The rearward thrust of a firearm caused by the reaction to the powder gases pushing the bullet through the bore.*

REVOLVER: *A multi-shot handgun, using a revolving cylinder as a cartridge container.*

RECOIL OPERATION: *An automatic or semi-automatic action in which barrel and breech are positively locked together during firing, but move rearward while locked until bore pressure has dropped enough to allow the action to open without blowing the case apart.*

R.F.: *Denotes "rimfire".*

RECOIL SPRING: *The spring or springs that returns the action into battery after the discharge of an automatic weapon.*

RIFLING: *Spiral grooves cut into the bore which impart a spin to the projectile to keep it point-on during flight.*

RIM: *The flange around the cartridge head which gives the extractor hook a hold.*

RIMFIRE: *That type of cartridge in which the priming mixture is housed in the rim.*

ROUND: *One cartridge per piece for a single shot. One round is one shot.*

R.N.: *Abbreviation for "round nose".*

Slide lock and magazine release button on Colt M1911 autoloader.

Rear sight, revolver (L) and auto (R) styles.

SEAR: *That part of a firing mechanism that holds the hammer or striker in the cocked position. When the sear is forced out of engagement by the trigger, the hammer falls and the gun fires.*

SHELL: *An explosive projectile fired from a cannon. Slang for small arms cartridge.*

SHOT: *The discharge of a firearm.*

SIDEARM: *A weapon which can be easily worn upon the person, leaving both hands free when not in use.*

SIGHT: *The device(s) used to align the shooter's eye as nearly as possible with the trajectory of a small arms projectile.*

Cylinder release, Colt (L) and Smith & Wesson (R) types.

SMALL ARMS: *In general, those arms intended to be carried and operated by one man. Specifically, any firearm of less than .50 caliber.*

SIGHT RADIUS: *The distance between the front and rear sight. The longer this distance, the more precise the alignment.*

S.P.: *Abbreviation for "soft point".*

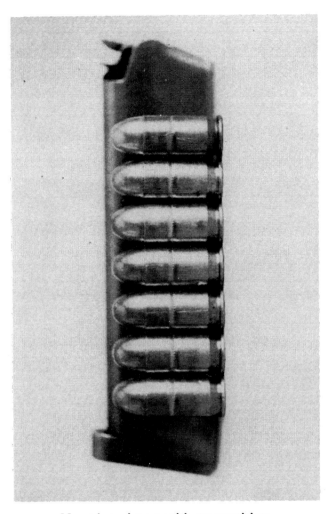

Magazine, shown with ammunition.

STOCK: *The wood or plastic portion of a small arm intended to be held by the hands and to support the recoil. Handgun stocks are usually two-piece, thus the plural.*

SMOKELESS POWDER: *Gun powder which gives off almost no smoke during combustion.*

STRIKER: *A firing element that moves in a straight line, as opposed to a hammer which swings in an arc.*

S.W.C.: *Abbreviation for "semi-wadcutter"*

TARGET: *The object of the act of shooting.*

TRAJECTORY: *The path of the projectile fired from a small arm.*

TRANSFER BAR: *A safety device used in modern handguns that prevents the hammer from contacting the firing pin, thus reducing the potential for accidental discharge.*

TRIGGER: *The finger piece of a small arm which, when pressed, allows the sear to drop away and the hammer to fall.*

TWIST: *Angle of rifling relative to the axis of the bore. Normally expressed in terms of turns or part-turns per inch.*

Machine Pistol. A self-loading gun with a selector switch allows fully automatic fire.

The first truly practical self-loading pistol, the M1896 Mauser "Broomhandle" as carried by Winston Churchill in the Battle of Omdurman, the first recorded instance of an autoloader being carried in combat.

TRIGGER COCKING: *That form of firing which utilizes trigger manipulation to cause the weapon to cock itself.*

W.C.: *Abbreviation for "wadcutter".*

VELOCITY: *Projectile speed, measured in feet-per-second. Faster at the muzzle and tapering off as distance from the muzzle increases.*

ZERO: *That sight setting which gives bullet group desired and from which subsequent changes in sight settings will be made.*

Handgun Nomenclature

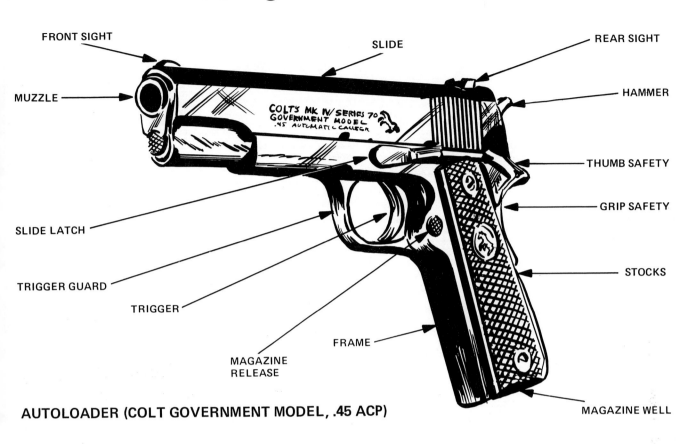

FRONT SIGHT

SLIDE

REAR SIGHT

MUZZLE

HAMMER

COLT'S MK IV/SERIES 70
GOVERNMENT MODEL
.45 AUTOMATIC CALIBER

THUMB SAFETY

GRIP SAFETY

SLIDE LATCH

STOCKS

TRIGGER GUARD

TRIGGER

FRAME

MAGAZINE
RELEASE

AUTOLOADER (COLT GOVERNMENT MODEL, .45 ACP)

MAGAZINE WELL

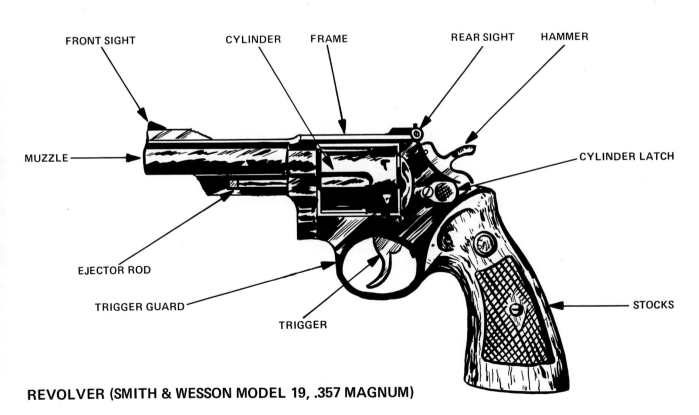

FRONT SIGHT

CYLINDER

FRAME

REAR SIGHT

HAMMER

MUZZLE

CYLINDER LATCH

EJECTOR ROD

TRIGGER GUARD

STOCKS

TRIGGER

REVOLVER (SMITH & WESSON MODEL 19, .357 MAGNUM)

Arms Importers & Manufacturers

ASTRA-UNCETA Y COMPANIA, S.A.
Guernica, Spain

AUTO-ORDNANCE CORPORATION
West Hurley, N.Y. 12491

BAUER FIREARMS CO.
345750 Klein Ave.
Fraser, MI

PIETRO BERETTA
Gardone, V.T.
Brescia, Italy

FRATTELLI BERNARDELLI
Brescia, Italy

BROWNING ARMS CO.
Route 1
Morgan, UT 84050

CHARTER ARMS CORP.
430 Sniffens Lane
Stratford, CT 06497

COLT INDUSTRIES
Colt's Firearms Division
150 Huyshope Ave.
Hartford, CT 06102

CONNECTICUT VALLEY ARMS
Higganum, CT 06441

DETONICS
Seattle, WA

ERMA-WERKE
Dachau, West Germany

FABRIQUE NATIONALE D'ARMES
DE GUERRE
Herstal, Liege, Belgium

FIREARMS CENTER, INC.
113 Spokane
Victoria, TX 77901
(MKE)

FIREARMS IMPORT & EXPORT CORP.
251 W. 22nd Ave.
Miami, FL 33135
(Taurus)

GARCIA CORP.
329 Alfred Ave.
Teaneck, NY 07666
(Rossi, Star, Astra)

GIL HEBARD GUNS
Knoxville, IL 61448

HAMMERLI
Lenzburg, Switzerland

HARRINGTON & RICHARDSON, INC.
320 Park Ave.
Worcester, MA 01610

HAWES FIREARMS
8224 W. Sunset Blvd.
Los Angeles, CA 90069

HECKLER & KOCH
Oberndorf am Neckar
West Germany

HIGH STANDARD MFG. CORP.
1817 Dixwell Ave.
Hamden, CT 06514

INTERARMS
10 Price St.
Alexandria VA 22313

IVER JOHNSON ARMS & CYCLE WORKS
Fitchburg, MA 01420

LLAMA
Gabilondo y Cia
Elgoibar, Spain

MAUSER AMERIKA
1721 Crooks Rd.
Troy, MI 48084

NORTH AMERICAN ARMS CORP.
Newbury Park, CA 91320

NORTON ARMAMENT CORP.
41471 Irwin
Mt. Clemens, MI 48043

REMINGTON ARMS CO., INC.
939 Barnum Ave.
Bridgeport, CT 06602

R.G. INDUSTRIES, INC.
2485 N.W. 20th St.
Miami, FL 33142

SCHWEIZERISHE INDUSTRIE
GESELLSHAFT (SIG)
Neuhausen am Reinfalls
Schaffhausen, Switzerland

SECURITY ARMS CO., INC.
1815 N. Fort Meyer Drive
Arlington, VA 22209

L.W. SEECAMP
New Haven, CT

SMITH & WESSON, INC.
2100 Roosevelt Ave.
Springfield, MA 01101

STAR-B ECHEVARRIA
Eibar, Spain

STERLING ARMS CORP.
2209 Elmwood Ave.
Buffalo, NY 14216

STEYR-DAIMLER-PUCH AKTIENGESELI-
SHAFT
Steyr Werke
Steyr, Austria

STOEGER ARMS CORP.
55 Ruta Court
South Hackensack, NJ 07606

STURM, RUGER & CO.
Lacey Place
Southport, CT 06490

THOMPSON/CENTER ARMS
Farmington Road
Rochester, NH 03867

UNIQUE MANUFACTURE D'ARMES
Des Pyrenees
Hendaye, France

UNIVERSAL FIREARMS CORP.
3746 E. 10th St.
Hialeah, FL 33013

CARL WALTHER WAFFENFABRIK
Ulm/Donau
West Germany

WEBLEY & SCOTT, LTD.
Parklane, Handsworth
Birmingham 21, England

DAN WESSON ARMS
293 Main St.
Monson, MA 01057

Accessories - Where To Find Them

AMMUNITION

Bingham, Ltd.
1175-C Wilwat Dr.
Norcross, GA 30093
(Exploder and Devastator
Ammunition)

Federal Cartridge Co.
2700 Fooshay Tower
Minneapolis, MN 55402

Frontier Cartridge Co.
Division of Hornady Mfg. Co.
Box 1848
Grand Island, NB 68801
(Full metal jacketed flat nose)

Glaser Safety Slug, Inc.
P.O. Box 1975
McAllen, TX 78501

H & H Cartridge Corp.
County Road, 200 W.
Box 104
Greensburg, IN 47240
(Super Vel)

K T W, Inc.
710 Foster Park Rd.
Lorain, OH 44053
(Metal Piercing Ammo)

Norma Precision
P.O. Box 30-06
Ithaca, NY 14850
(Ammo, unprimed brass)

Omark-CCI, Inc.
Box 856
Lewiston, ID 83501

Remington Arms Co.
Bridgeport, CT 06602

Velet Cartridge Co.
N. 6809 Lincoln
Spokane, WA 99208

Winchester-Western
East Alton, IL 62024

BULLETS & RELOADS

American Ballistics Co.
P.O. Box 1410
Marietta, GA 30061
(Reloaded ammo)

Atlanta Arms & Ammo
6721 Covington Hwy.
Lithonia, GA 30058
(Reloads)

Brocks
P.O. Box 236
Stone Mountain, GA 30083
(Cast bullets)

Collins Custom Actions
Rt. 1, Box 17, Marion Oaks
Tuscaloosa, AL 35405
(Bullets, reloads)

Hornady Mfg. Co.
Box 1848
Grand Island, NB 68801
(Factory ammo, bullets for
reloading

Sierra Bullets, Inc.
10532 Painter Ave.
Santa Fe Springs, CA 90670
(Bullets)

Speer Products, Inc.
Box 896
Lewiston, ID 83501

G/S Munitions, Inc.
Rt. 1, Box 59D
Hereford, AZ 85615
(Reloads)

Crockett's
9699 Webb St.
Elk Grove, CA 95624
(Hard cast bullets)

Castaway Bullet Co.
P.O. Box 259
East Palestine, OH 44413
(Cast bullets)

GUN CARE & CLEANING PRODUCTS

Belding and Mull
P.O. Box 428
Philipsburg, PA 16866
(Cleaning kits, tools)

Belltown Distributors
P.O. Box 444
Bedford Hills, NY 10507
(Gun cleaning cloth kit wipes
away lead build-up)

Durango, U.S.A.
P.O. Box 1029
Durango, CO 81301
(Cleaning rods)

Electrofilm, Inc.
7116 Laurel Canyon Blvd.
North Hollywood, CA 91605
(Gun lubricant)

Fluoramics, Inc.
103 Pleasant Ave.
Upper Saddle River, NJ 07458
(Tufoil Gun Coat Gun Lubricant)

LEM Gun Specialties, Inc.
P.O. Box 31
College Park, GA 30337
(Lewis Lead Remover)

Kleen Bore
Yankee Hill Machine Co., Inc.
Northhampton, MA 01060

M.G.O.
P.O. Box 2178
Adison, NJ 08817
(Cleaning patches)

Numrich Arms Co.
West Hurley, NY 12491
(Gun blue)

Outers Laboratories, Inc.
P.O. Box 39
Onalaska, WI 54650
(Cleaning kits)

Penguin Industries, Inc.
Airport Industrial Mall
Coatsville, PA 19320
(Hoppe's solvent and oil)

RIG Products Co.
Division of Mitann
21320 Deering Court
Canoga Park, CA 91304

FINISHES

Devel Corp.
3441 West Brainard Rd.
Cleveland, OH 44122
(Hard chrome & matte nickel)

Marker Machine Co.
Box 426
Charleston, IL 61920
(Black chrome)

Metalife
P.O. Box 53
Mong Ave.
Reno, PA 16343

Metaloy Co., Inc.
6567 E. 21st Pl.
Tulsa, OK 74129
(Hard satin finish,
70 Rockwell "C")

Nitex
600 N. Glenville
Richardson, TX 75091

HEARING PROTECTORS

Acoustical Research, Inc.
Environmental (Insta) Mold
P. O. Box 2146
Boulder, CO 80306

Bausch & Lomb
635 St. Paul St.
Rochester, NY 14602

David Clark Co., Inc.
360 Franklin St.
Worcester, MA 01604

E.A.R. Corp.
7911 Zionsville Rd.
Indianapolis, IN 46268

Flints Products Co., Inc.
14 Orchard St.
Norwalk, CT 06850
(Silenta hearing protector,
Flexiplug ear protector,
Silafex ear protector)

Norton Co.
Safety Products Div.
1662 Edwards Rd.
Arritos, CA 90701
(Sonics II)

Safety Direct, Inc.
23 Snider Way
Sparks, NV 89431

Sportmuff Sales Co., Inc.
37 Tripps Lane
East Providence, RI 02915

Wilson Safety Products Div.
P.O. Box 622
Reading, PA 19603

LEATHER

Alessi
2465 Niagara Falls Blvd.
Tonawanda, NY 14150
(Send $2.00 for catalog)

American Sales & Mfg. Co.
P.O. Box 677
Laredo, TX 78040
(Holsters & gun belts)

Armament Systems Products,
Unlimited
P.O. Box 18595 - CH
Atlanta, GA 30326

Belt Slide, Inc.
Box 15303
Austin, TX 78761

Bianchi Holster Co.
100 Calle Cortez
Temecula, CA 92390
(Send $1.00 for catalog)

Ted Blocker's Custom Holsters
P.O. Box 821
Rose Mead, CA 91770
(Send $1.00 for catalog)

Brauer Bros. Mfg. Co.
2012 Washington
St. Louis, MO 63103
(Holsters, belts & gun cases)

Bucheimer & Bucheimer Clark
P.O. Box 280
Frederick, MD 21701
(Holsters, belts & pistol cases)

Cobra, Ltd.
1865 New Highway
Farmingdale, NY 11735
(Send $1.00 for catalog)

El Paso Saddlery
P.O. Box 27194
El Paso, TX 79926

G. Wm. Davis
P.O. Box 446
Arcadia, CA 91006
(Send $2.00 for catalog)

Gene Desantis
1601 Jericho Turnpike
New Hyde Park, N.Y. 11040
(Send $1.00 for catalog)

Hanson's Holsters
2724 N.W. Keel
Lincoln City, OR 97367

Steve Henigson
2049 Kerwood Ave., No. 3
Los Angeles, CA 90025

Don Hume Leather Goods
Box 351
Miami, OK 74354

Jackass Leather
7383 North Rodgers Ave.
Chicago, IL 60626

The George Lawrence Co.
306 S.W. First Ave.
Portland, OR 97204

Pete Mason
The Armoury, R.R. 2
Bluffton, Alberta
TOC OMO
Canada

Kenneth L. Null Custom Holsters
R.D. No. 5, Box 197
Hanover, PA 17331
(Send $3.00 for catalog)

Rogers Holsters
10701 Theresa Dr.
Jacksonville, FL 32216

Roy's Custom Leather
Hwy. 1325 & Rawhide Rd.
Magnolia, AR 71753

Thad Rybka, Custom Leather
Maker
Rt. 1, Box 446
Odenville, AL 35120
(Send $3.00 for catalog)

Leathersmiths, Inc.
350 N. Lantana Ave., Suite 504
Camarillo, CA 93010

Smith & Wesson
2100 Roosevelt Ave.
Springfield, MA 01101

Milt Sparks
Box 187
Idaho City, ID 83631
(Send $2.00 for catalog)

Robert A. Strong Co., Inc.
105 Maplewood Ave.
Gloucester, MA 01930
(Holsters & Belts)

Triple K Mfg. Co.
568 Sixth Ave.
San Diego, CA 92101

Snick Products Mfg.
W and W Machine Co.
3212 Gulf St.
Bakersfield, CA 93308
(Send $1.00 for catalog)

Pistol Clip Belt
Browne & Pharr Mfg. Co.
1775-1 Wilwat Dr.
Norcross, GA 30693

MAGAZINES

Bingham, Ltd.
1775-C Wilwat Dr.
Norcross, GA 30093

D & E
P.O. Box 4579
Downey, CA 90242

Laka Industries
P.O. Box 837
Westbury, Long Island,
N.Y. 11590

Pacific International Merchandising Corp.
2215 "J" St.
Sacramento, CA 93818
(Vega)

MOUNTS & BASES

Brownell's, Inc.
Route 2, Box 1
Montezume, IA 50171
(Send $3.00 for catalog)

Maynard P. Buehler, Inc.
Orinda, CA 94563
(Pistol mounts & bases)

Conetrol
Hwy. 123 South
Seguin, TX 78155
(Pistol mounts and bases)

Whitney
P.O. Box 875
Reseda, CA 91335

PARTS, BARRELS, MAGAZINE PADS & ACCESSORIES

Arcadia Machine & Tool
11666 McBean Dr.
El Monte, CA 91732

Bar-sto Precision Machine
633 S. Victory Blvd.
Burbank, CA 91502
(S.S. barrels, link, pin &
bushing)

Crown City Arms
P.O. Box 1126
Cortland, N.Y. 13045
(.45 frames)

Essex Arms
Box 345
Phaering St.
Island Port, VT 05864
(.45 frames)

Jack First Distributors, Inc.
44633 Sierra Hwy.
Lancaster, CA 93534
(Gun parts, tools &
accessories)

Jim's Flye Shoppe
Rd. No. 1, 9518 Route 60
Fredonia, NY 14063
(Extended magazine release
button)

L. H. Green Co.
Rt. 1, Box 210
Devine, TX 78016
(National Match .45 auto
barrels, parts)

H & D Products
8534 Canoga Ave.
Canoga Park, CA
(Extended slide stops, extended
speed safety, high visibility combat fixed sights, wide grip safety,
magazine base pads)

Hamrick's Gunsmithing
817 Montague Ave.
Greenwood, SC 29646
(Grip safety locks)

Hi Quality Enterprises
6311 Yucca St.
Box 1083
Los Angeles, CA 90038
(Loaded chamber indicator)

Laka Tool Co.
62 Kimkel St.
Westbury, Long Island,
NY 11590
(Stainless steel .45 auto parts)

Micro Sight Co.
242 Harron Blvd.
Belmont, CA 94002

Natchez Shooters Supplies
P.O. Box 17591-A
Nashville, TN 37217
(.45 parts & accessories)

Numrich Arms Corp.
Williams Lane
West Hurley, NY 12491
(Parts, formula 44/40 gun
bluing agent)

Oaks
954 Florida Ave.
Rockledge FL 32955
(.45 frames)

Pacific International
Merchandising
2215 "J" St.
Sacramento, CA 95818)
(.45 frames, parts)

Robbins
P.O. Box 504
St. Charles, IL 60174
(Send $1.00 for catalog)

Rock Island Armory
111 E. Exchange St.
Genesco, IL 61254
(.45 forms, parts)

Safari Arms
P.O. Box 28355
Tempe, AZ 85252
(Extended slide stop)

Shootist Supply
622 5th St.
Belle Fourche, SD 57717
(Colt parts)

Silva Products
614 South Gold
P.O. Drawer 270
Deming, NM 88030
(Silva hammers)

Texas Armament Co.
P.O. Box 135
Brownwood, TX 76801
(Most all parts for .45)

Wilson's Gun Shop
Route 3, Box 211-D
Berryville, AR 72616
(Send two (2) 20 cent
stamps for brochure)

Sarco, Inc.
323 Union St.
Stirling, NJ 07980
(Most .45 parts)

Federal Ordnance, Inc.
1443 Potrero Ave., South
El Monte, CA 91733
Taylor 30 rd. drum)

RELOADING EQUIPMENT

Bonanza Sports Mfg. Co.
412 Western Ave.
Faribault, MN 55021

CPM Industries Corp.
P.O. Box 468
Norwalk, OH 44857
(Progressive reloader)

Camdex, Inc.
2228 14 Mile Rd.
Warren, MI 48092
(Hand and automatic reloading
equipment)

Dillon Precision Products, Inc.
7755 E. Gelding Dr.
Suite 106
Scottsdale, AZ 85260
(Progressive reloader)

Hensley & Gibbs
Box 10
Murphy, OR 97533
(Bullets, molds)

Lee Precision, Inc.
Hartford, WI 53027
(Bullet molds, production pot)

RCBS, Inc.
Box 1919
Oroville, CA 93965

SAECO Reloading, Inc.
525 Maple St.
Cerpinteria, CA 93013

Tru-Square Metal Products
640 First St. SW
Auburn, WA 98002
(Case polishers & accessories)

Quinetics Corp.
5731 Kenwick
P.O. Box 29007
San Antonio, TX 78238
(Kinetic bullet puller, automatic
shell holder, powder measure)

SAFETIES

Colt Firearms
150 Huyshope Ave.
Hartford, CT 06102

Swenson's .45 Shop
P.O. Box 606
Fallbrook, CA 92028

SCOPES

Bushnell
2828 E. Foothill Blvd.
Pasadena, CA 91107

Fontaine Industries, Inc.
11552 Knott St., Suite 2
Garden Grove, CA 92641

Leupold & Stevens
P.O. Box 688
Beaverton, OR 97005

Tasco
1075 N.W. 71st St.
Miami, FL 33138

Thompson/Center
P.O. Box 2405
Rochester, N.H. 03867

SPRING KITS

Trapper Gun, Inc.
28019 St. Clair Shores, MI 48081
(Bulls Eye Spring Kits)

SIGHTS & INSERTS

Bo-Mar
Box 168
Carthage, TX 75633
(Adjustable sights)

Gutridge, Inc.
533 214th St.
Dyer, IN 46311
(Quickline Combat Sight)

Lee's Red Ramps
7252 E. Ave.
Littlerock, CA 93543
(Red ramp kits and white outline
rear sight blades)

Micro Sight
242 Harbor Blvd.
Belmont, CA 94002
(Adjustable/fixed sights)

Millet Industries
16131 Gothard St.
Huntington Beach, CA 92647
(Millet Mark II fixed sight —
carries an unlimited lifetime
warranty)

Miniature Machine Co.
210 E. Poplar
Deming, NM 88030
(MMC adjustable pistol sights)

Nite Site, Inc.
P.O. Box 0
Rosemont, MN 55068

Omega Sales, Inc.
P.O. Box 1066
Mt. Clemens, MI 48043

Precision Riflex, Inc.
201 N. Main St.
New Bremen, OH 45869
(Insta-sight)

Travis Strahan
Rt. 7, Townsend Cir.
Ringold, GA 30736
(Mascott III adjustable sight)

Handgun Related Materials (Publications): Volumes Of Knowledge

Blue Steel & Gun Leather
By John Bianchi
Beinfeld Publishing Co.
North Hollywood, CA

Book of Pistols and Revolvers
W. H. B. Smith
Stackpole Books
Harrisburg, PA

Browning Hi—Power Pistols
Anubus Press
Houston, TX

Colt Automatic Pistols
Donald B. Bady
Borden Publishing Co.
Alhambra, CA

The Colt .45 Auto Pistol
Desert Publications
Cornville, AZ

Combat Handgun Shooting
James D. Mason
Charles C. Thomas
Springfield, IL

Combat Handguns
Maj. George C. Nonte, Jr.
Stackpole Books
Harrisburg, PA

Combat Shooting for Police
Paul B. Weston
Charles C. Thomas
Springfield, IL

The Complete Handgun — 1300 to the Present
Ian V. Hogg
John Batchelor
Exeter Books
New York, NY

Defensive Handgun Effectiveness
Carroll E. Peters
Manchester, TN

Famous Automatic Pistols & Revolvers
John Olson
Jolex Books
Oakland, NJ

German Pistols & Revolvers: 1871-1945
Ian V. Hogg
A & W Books
New York, N.Y.

GUNS Annual Book of Handguns
Jerome Rakusan
Publishers Development Corp.
San Diego, CA

A Handbook of the Primary Identification of Revolvers and Semi-Automatic Pistols
John T. Millard
Charles C. Thomas
Springfield, IL

The Handgun
Geoffrey Boothroyd
Outlet Publishing Co.
New York, NY

Handgun Competition
Maj. George C. Nonte, Jr.
Winchester Press
New York, N.Y.

Handguns Americana
DeWitt Sell
Borden Publishing Co.
Alhambra, CA

Japanese Handguns
F. E. Leithe
Borden Publishing Co.
Alhambra, CA

Cooper on Handguns
Jeff Cooper
Peterson Publishing Co.
Los Angeles, CA

Know Your .45 Auto Pistols
E. J. Hoffschmidt
Blacksmith Corp.
Stamford, CT

Know Your Walther P-38 Pistols
E. J. Hoffschmidt
Blacksmith Corp.
Stamford, CT

Law Enforcement Handgun Digest
3rd Edition
Dean A. Grennell
DBI Books, Inc.
Northfield, IL

The Luger Pistol
F. A. Datig
Borden Publishing Co.
Alhambra, CA

Mauser Pocket Pistols: 1910-1946
Roy G. Pender
Collector's Press
Houston, TX

The Mauser Self Loading Pistol
Belford & Dunlap
Borden Publishing Co.
Alhambra, CA

The Military Four
Claude V. Holland
C. V. Holland
Bonita Springs, FL

Military Pistols and Revolvers
I. V. Hogg
Arco Publishing Co.
New York, NY

The Modern Handgun
Robert Hertzberg
A & W Books
New York, N.Y.

The Official U.S. Army Pistol Marksmanship Guide
J & A Publishing Co.
New York, N.Y.

The Original Mauser Automatic Pistol
Harold C. Bruffett
Croswell, MI

The Parabellum Automatic Pistol
Stoeger Publishing Co.
Hackensack, N.J.

The Pistol Guide
Maj. George C. Nonte, Jr.
Stoeger Publishing Co.
Hackensack, N.J.

Pistol and Revolver Digest
Dean A. Grennell
Jack Lewis
DBI Books
Northfield, IL

Pistol & Revolver Guide
Maj. George C. Nonte, Jr.
Follett Publishing Co.
Chicago, IL

Pistols: A Modern Encyclopedia
Henry M. Stebbins
Castle Books
New York, N.Y.

Pistols of the World
Ian V. Hogg
John Weeks
Arms & Armour Press
London

Quick or Dead
William Cassidy
Paladin Press
Boulder, CO

Report of the Board on Tests of Revolvers and Automatic Pistols
J. C. Tilling
Marlow, N.H.

Shooting to Live with the One-Hand Gun
Wm. E. Fairbairn
Eric A. Sykes
Paladin Press
Boulder, CO

Principal Military Handguns Of The World

Nation	Weapon	Caliber	Type	Cap.	Bbl.	Wgt.
ARGENTINA	Browning Hi-Power	9mm Luger	S-A	13	5	32
	Ballester Molina	.45 ACP	S-A	7	5	40
	Mannlicher M-1905	7.63mm Mannlicher	S-A	10	6.2	32
AUSTRIA	Steyr M-12	9mm Steyr	S-A	8	5	34
	Roth-Steyr M-07	8mm R-S	S-A	1-	5.1	34
	Rast-Gasser	8mm R-G	R	8	4.5	33
BELGIUM	Browning Hi-Power	9mm Luger	S-A	13	5	32
	Browning M-1903	9mm Br. Long	S-A	7	5	30
	Browning M-1900	7.65mm Browning	S-A	7	4	22
BRITAIN	Browning Hi-Power	9mm Luger	S-A	13	5	32
	Enfield	.380/200	R	6	5	28
	Webley	.455	R	6	4-6	38
	Webley M-1913	.455 Auto	S-A	7	5	36
CZECHOSLOVAKIA	Cz M-52	7.62mm Russian	S-A	8	4.7	25
	Cz M-50	7.65mm Browning	S-A	8	3.8	24
	Cz M-38	9mm Br. Short	S-A	8	4.6	33
	Cz M-27	7.65mm Browning	S-A	8	3.5	25
	Cz M-22 & M-24	9mm Br. Short	S-A	8	3.5	24
DENMARK	Browning Hi-Power	9mm Luger	S-A	13	5	32
	Bergmann M-10	9mm Bayard	S-A	6-10	4	36
FRANCE	M-1950	9mm Luger	S-A	9	4.4	29
	M-1935A & S	7.65mm Long	S-A	8	4.3	26
	Lebel M-92	8mm Lebel	R	6	4	31
	Service M-73	11mm French Service	R	6	4.2	39
GERMANY	Walther P-38	9mm Luger	S-A	8	4.8	34
	Luger M-08	9mm Luger	S-A	8	4.6	30
	Mauser M-96	9mm Luger	S-A	10	5.3	45
	Service M-79	10.6 (11)mm	R	6	5	37
HUNGARY	Model 48	7.65mm Browning	S-A	8	4	24
	Frommer M-39	7.65mm & 9mm Br. Short	S-A	7	3.3	22
ITALY	Beretta M-51	9mm Luger	S-A	8	4.5	31
	Beretta M-34	9mm Br. Short & 7.65mm	S-A	7	3.5	24
	Glisenti M-10	9mm Glisenti	S-A	7	4	32
	Service M-72	10.35mm Italian Service	R	6	6.3	33
JAPAN	Nambu Type 14	8mm Nambu	S-A	8	4.5	30
	Type 26 (M-1893)	9mm Japanese	R	6	4.7	32
MEXICO	Obregon	.45 ACP	S-A	7	5	39

Nation	Weapon	Caliber	Type	Cap.	Bbl.	Wgt.
POLAND	Radom M-35	9mm Luger	S-A	8	4.8	30
SPAIN	Astra M-400	9mm Bayard	S-A	8	5.5	32
	Campo-Giro	9mm Bayard	S-A	8	6.7	33
	Bergmann-Bayard	9mm Bayard	S-A	6-10	4	36
SWEDEN	Lahti M-40	9mm Luger	S-A	8	5.5	36
	FN Browning M-07	9mm Browning (.380)	S-A	7	5	32
	Nagant M-87	7.5mm	R	6	4.5	28
SWITZERLAND	Neuhausen M-49 (SIG)	9mm Luger	S-A	8	4.7	34
	Luger M-1900	7.65mm Luger	S-A	8	4	30
	Army Model 1882	7.5mm	R	6	5	30
RUSSIA	Makarov M-PM	9mm Makarov	S-A	8	3.8	26
	Stechkin-APS	9mm Makarov	S-A	20	5	30
	Tokarev TT 30 & 33	7.62mm Tokarev	S-A	8	4.5	33
	Nagant M-95	7.62mm Nagant	R	7	4.5	28
UNITED STATES	Colt M-1911 & M-1911A1	.45 ACP	S-A	7	5	39
	Colt M-1917	.45 ACP	R	6	5.5	40
	S&W M-1917	.45 ACP	R	6	5.5	37
	Colt New Service-09	.45 Colt 1909	R	6	6	40
	Colt Army & Navy-92	.38 Long Colt	R	6	6	34
	S&W Army M-1875	.45 S&W	R	6	7	38
	Colt SA Army M-1873	.45 Colt	R	6	7.5	40

NOTE: Only the principal or official model is listed. Most governments used a variety of alternate types and officers often used non-official arms. The latest model is always listed first, older models in order.

S-A = Semi-Auto; R = Revolver
Cap. = Cylinder or magazine capacity

CUSTOM GUNSMITH DIRECTORY:
Men Who Understand The Combat Handgun

Alabama

Walker Arms Co.
Route 2, Box 73
Selma, AL 37601
(205) 872-3888

Arkansas

Wilson's Gun Shop
101-103 Public Square
Berryville, AR 72616
(501) 423-2982

California

Centaur Systems
1653 South Magnolia Ave.
Monrovia, CA 91016
(213) 357-2645

F. Bob Chow
3185 Mission Street
San Francisco, CA 94110

Keith Hamilton
P.O. Box 871
Gridley, CA 95948
(916) 846-3968

James W. Hoag
8523 Canoga Avenue
Suite C
Canoga Park, CA 91304
(213) 998-1510

King's Gun Works
1837 West Glenoaks Road
Glendale, CA 91201
(213) 244-6811

Pachmayr Gun Works
1220 South Grand Avenue
Los Angeles, CA 90015
(213) 748-7271

Robert A. Richter
5792 Vista de Oro
Riverside, CA 92509

Chuck Ries
P.O. Box 205
Culver City, CA 90203
(213) 837-6858

Earl R. Stroup
30506 Flossmoor Way
Hayward, CA 94544
(415) 471-1549

Swenson's .45 Shop
3839 Ladera Vista
Box 606
Fallbrook, CA 92028

Colorado

Don Fisher
2199 Kitteridge Way
Aurora, CO 80013
(303) 755-3710

Dominic DiStefano
4303 Friar Lane
Colorado Springs, CO 80907

Sports West, Inc.
2200 W. Alameda Avenue
Denver, CO 80223
(303) 934-4466

"300" Gunsmith Service
4655 Washington Street
Denver, CO 80216
(303) 893-2158

Connecticut

Colt Custom Gun Shop
150 Huyshope Avenue
Hartford, CT 06102

L. W. Seecamp
Box 255
New Haven, CT 06502

Florida

Gateway Shooters Supply
SDR Custom Handguns
10145 103rd Street
Jacksonville, FL 32210
(904) 778-2277

Reed Knight
1306 29th
Vero Beach, FL 32960

Georgia

Bill Hayllar
Atlanta Firearms
285 Mt. Vernon Highway
Atlanta, GA 30328
(404) 256-GUNS

Bullseye Gunshop
5091-F Buford Highway
Doraville, GA 30340
(404) 455-4543

Travis R. Strahan
Route 7
Ringold, GA 30736
(404) 937-4495

Smith & Wood
605 West Currahee Street
Toccoa, GA 30577
(404) 886-5792

Illinois

Richard Heinie
821 East Adams
Havana, IL 62644
(309) 543-4535

Harold Shockley
Box 116
Hanna City, IL 61536
(309) 565-4524

Dennis Ulrich
2511 South 57th Avenue
Cicero, IL 60650

Indiana

Jack Gutridge
533 214th St.
Dyer, IN 46311
(219) 865-8617

Iowa

Fred R. Miller
2620 East 32nd Street
Davenport, IA 52807
(319) 356-6165

Kansas

Duane Hobbie
2412 Pattie
Wichita, KS 67216

Louisiana

James E. Clark
Route 2, Box 22A
Keithsville, LA 71047
(318) 925-0836

Ken Eversull
P.O. Box 1766
Alexandria, LA 71301
(318) 442-0569

Maryland

Maryland Gun Works
26200 Frederick Road
Hyattstown, MD 20734
(301) 874-2661

Alan Marvel
3922 Madonna Road
Jarrettsville, MD 21804
(301) 557-7270

Michigan

Trapper Gun, Inc.
28019 Harper
St. Claire Shores, MI 48081
(313) 779-8750

Mag-Na-Port Arms
30016 South River Road
Mt. Clemens. MI 48045
(313) 469-6727

The Sho-Gun Shop
26646 Five Mile Road
Redford, MI 48239
(313)535-0819/534-3272

Michigan Armamant, Inc.
214 East Adrian Street
Blissfield, MI 49228
(517) 486-4000

Moran Custom Guns
2275 E. Farrand Road
Clio, MI 49228

Minnesota

JJL Custom Guns
1333 Highland Parkway
St. Paul, MN 55116
(612) 690-1333

Missouri

Nu-Line Guns
1053 Caulks Hill Road
Harvester, MO 63301
(314) 441-4500/447-4501

Montana

Cannon's Guns
P.O. Box 357, Route 93
Victor, MT 59875

Nebraska

Cylinder and Slide Shop
523 North Main Street
P.O. Box 937
Fremont, NE 68025
(402) 721-4277

New Hampshire

Silver Dollar Guns
10 Francis Street
Franklin, N.H. 03235

Vic's Gun Refinishing
6 Pineview Dr. Dover Pt.
Dover, N.H. 03820

New Jersey

Behlert Custom Guns
725 Lehigh Avenue
Union, N.J. 07083
(201) 687-3438

Joe K's, Inc.
500 High Street
Perth Amboy, N.J. 08861
(201) 442-4114

New York

Crawford's Gunsmithing
Swain Drive
Pleasant Valley, N.Y. 12569
(914) 635-3210

Ohio

Cleveland Blueing Co.
1024 East 185th Street
Cleveland, OH 44119
(216) 481-2104

Schneider Gunsmithing
404 W. Garbry Road
Piqua, OH 45356
(513) 773-1417

Oklahoma

Steve Vaniadis
4657 East 57th Place
Tulsa, OK 74135
(918) 496-2074

Ammo Data, .45 ACP & 9mm Parabellum

.45 ACP SERVICE AMMUNITION

The following cartridges are intended for use in both the M1911A1 service pistol and the M3A1 submachine gun unless otherwise noted.

M1911 BALL
BALLISTICS:
Velocity: 855 + 25 fps at 25.5 feet.
Pressure: 19,000 psi, max. avg.
Accuracy: 7.46" diagonal (max. avg.) at 50 yards.

CARTRIDGE: 331 - 17 grs.
Case.   87 - 10 grs.
Bullet: 234 - 6 grs. copper alloy, 231 grs. gilding metal clad steel.
Propellant: SR7970, single base, flake, 5 grs., HPC-1, double base, flake, 5 grs.
Point Identification: Plain tip.

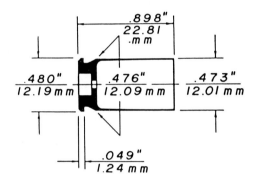

.45 ACP case dimensions.

M1911 STEEL CASE
BALLISTICS:
Velocity: 855 + or - 25 fps at 25.5 feet.
Pressure: 19,000 psi, max. avg.
Accuracy: 7.46" diagonal (max. avg.) at 50 yards.

CARTRIDGE: 321 - 20 grs.
Case: 82 - 10 grs.
Bullet: 234 - 6 grs.
Propellant: SR7970, single base, flake, 5 grs., HPC-1, double base, flake, 5 grs.

M1911 BALL, MATCH GRADE
WEAPON: M1911A1 National Match Pistol.

BALLISTICS:
Velocity: 855 + or - 25 fps at 25.5 feet.
Pressure: 19,000 psi, max. avg.
Accuracy: 3" diagonal (max. avg.) at 50 yards.

CARTRIDGE: 334 - 17 grs.
Case: 87 - 10 grs.

Bullet: 234 - 6 grs.
Propellant: SR7970, single base, flake, 5 grs., HPC-1, double base, flake, 5 grs.
Identification: Special head stamping "Match" or "NM".

M1 HIGH PRESSURE TEST
WEAPON: Used to proof test barrels and weapons (not a service cartridge).

BALLISTICS:
Pressure: 22,000 psi, max. avg.

CARTRIDGE: 334 - 17 grs.
Case: 87 - 10 grs.
Bullet: 234 - 6 grs.
Primer: Lead styphnate.
Propellant: SR7970, single base, flake, 7 grs., HPC-1, double base, flake, 7 grs.
Identification: Stannic stained case.

M9 BLANK
BALLISTICS:
Screen Perforation: 0.1" dia. max. perforations in screen at 15 feet.

CARTRIDGE: 104 grs. approx.
Primer: Lead styphnate.
Propellant: SR4990, single base, flake, 10 grs.,
Identification: No bullet, case mouth tapered and sealed with a red lacquered disk.

M9 STEEL CASE BLANK
Same as M9 Blank above except:
Cartridge weight: 91 grs.
Case: Steel, 85 - 10 grs.
Propellant: 7 grs.

M26 TRACER
BALLISTICS:
Velocity: 885 + or - 25 fps at 25.5 feet.
Pressure: 19,000 psi, max. avg.
Trace: Visible trace between 15 and 150 yards min.

CARTRIDGE: 331 - 17 grs.
Bullet: 203 grs. approx.
Tracer Composition: 3 grs. approx.
Igniter Composition: 2.5 grs. approx.
Primer: Lead styphnate.
Propellant: SR7970, single base, flake, 5 grs., HPC-1, double base, flake, 5 grs.
Point Identification: Red lacquer.

M26 STEEL CASE TRACER
Same as M26 above except:
Case weight: 82 - 10 grs.

.45 MATCH WADCUTTER (Commercial)
WEAPON: M1911A1 National Match Pistol.

BALLISTICS:

Velocity: The mean velocity of 10 rounds at 15 feet from the muzzle of the gun shall be 765 + or - 45 fps.

Pressure: The mean pressure of 10 rounds shall not exceed 18,000 psi. The extreme variation shall not exceed 6200 psi.

Accuracy: Average extreme spread of 5 - 5 shot targets at 50 yards shall not exceed 3.0 inches.

CARTRIDGE:

Case: Brass.
Bullet: 185 grs. gilding metal.
Propellant: Commercial.
Primer: Commercial lead styphnate.
Identification: Head stamp in accordance with commercial practice.

M1921 DUMMY CARTRIDGE

BALLISTICS: None.

CARTRIDGE: 313 grs. approx.
Bullet: 234 - 6 grs.
Identification: Hole in side wall of case.

M1921 STEEL CASE DUMMY CARTRIDGE

Same as M1921 Dummy above except:
Cartridge weight: 301 grs. approx.
Case: Steel, 82 - 10 grs.

FN 9mm P SERVICE AMMUNITION

The two cartridges listed below are intended for use in the wide variety of service pistols and submachine guns chambered for the 9mm Parabellum, the most conspicuous examples of each weapon class being, of course, the Browning P35 and the Uzi. However, these are by no means the only 9mm weapons in wide use throughout the world.

BALL

TECHNICAL DATA:
Cartridge: Length: 29.70mm.
Weight: 12.04 g.
Projectile: Weight: 8 g.

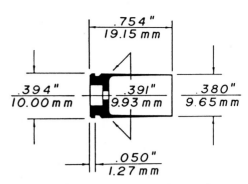

9mm Parabellum case dimensions.

BALLISTIC DATA:
Cartridge approved by NATO.
Muzzle velocity: 356 mps (meters per second).
Velocity at 12.5 m.: 336 mps.
(With Browning P35, barrel length 4-21/32".)
Chamber pressure (crusher): 2,856 bars max.
Muzzle energy: 507 J (1 J = 1 mkg x 9.806).

COMPONENTS:
Primer: oxyless, non-corrosive.
Case: brass 70/30.
Projectile: Core: lead; jacket: brass or nickeled brass.
Powder: Single or double base.

SPECIAL FEATURES:
At 15 meters, the round can pierce 5 mild steel plates 1mm thick, located 5 cm apart.

BLANK

(Automatic fire is possible in SMG's if they are fitted with a blank firing device.)
TECHNICAL DATA:
Cartriddge: Length: 29mm.
Weight: 5 g.

COMPONENTS:
Primer: oxyless, non-corrosive.
Case: brass 70/30.
Powder: double base.

SPECIAL FEATURES:
In a weapon fitted with a blank firing device, none of the fired rounds can pierce a paper target .10mm thick at a distance of 5 meters.

The newspaper editorial which appears below is a sad commentary on the times, indicating that about the only protection from violence the individual can expect is what he or she provides for himself or herself. This can take the form of many protective measures, from deadbolt locks and guard dogs to intensive training in the martial arts and in firearm use, as outlined in the previous pages. For those who question the value of firearms in the hands of private citizens, we need only show them the crime statistics from Kennesaw, Georgia, a community which *requires* the head of every household to own a gun and ammunition for it (with the exception of those who are legally forbidden to possess firearms or who oppose them on moral or religious grounds). Since Kennesaw passed its "armed citizen" ordinance, major crime has been reduced *drastically* in that community. We would like to give credit to the newspaper in which this editorial appeared, but unfortunately the person who sent it to us neglected to note its source. So we simply say a heartfelt "thank you" to an anonymous editorial writer and his courageous editor somewhere out there.

Police Have No "Duty" To Protect Individual

An appellate court in Washington, D.C., has ruled that the D.C. police department was not negligent in failing to protect three women from a brutal 14-hour ordeal in which they were repeatedly raped and beaten by two knife-wielding assailants.

The case stemmed from a 1975 incident in which two men broke into the house shared by the three women and a four-year-old child. Two of the women called the police after hearing the third woman's screams for help.

A police dispatcher assured them assistance was on the way. But one squad car arriving on the scene merely circled the house without stopping and another officer apparently knocked on the door but left when no one answered. The women telephoned police a second time, but according to the court record, the dispatcher failed to relay the second call.

The two intruders subsequently discovered the other women and abducted all three at knifepoint, repeatedly raping and beating them over the next 14 hours.

Even though two of the women had called the police and received assurances of assistance shortly before the crime occurred, the court said the women were not entitled to sue the police department for negligence.

In dismissing the women's suit, a seven-judge panel of the District of Columbia Court of Appeals reaffirmed what it called the "well established" and "uniformly accepted rule" that "a government and its agents are under no general duty to provide public services, such as police protection, to any particular individual citizen."

The court held that the police have a duty only "to the public at large and not to individual members of the community."

Similar court decisions across the nation place citizens in a dilemma. More and more states are adopting stronger limitations on the citizen's right of self-defense and on when an individual can use deadly force against a criminal assailant.

Compounding this is the nationwide drive at both the local and state levels by anti-gun groups to place increasingly restrictive gun laws on the books, laws which hamper the law-abiding citizen's efforts to possess firearms, especially handguns, for self-protection.

In the District, for example, handguns are virtually banned. Long guns kept in the home are required to be unassembled or trigger locked . . .

If higher court rulings ultimately hold that police have no duty to protect the individual citizen, and if the private ownership of firearms faces ever-increasing restraints, U.S. citizens will continue to find themselves at the mercy of the violence-prone criminal element.